BARRON'S BOOK NOTES

J. R. R. TOLKIEN'S

The Hobbit & The Lord of the Rings

BY

Anne M. Pienciak

SERIES COORDINATOR

Murray Bromberg
Principal, Wang High School of Queens
Holliswood, New York

Past President
High School Principals Association of New York City

BARRON'S EDUCATIONAL SERIES, INC.

To Walt

All inquiries should be addressed to:
Barron's Educational Series, Inc.
250 Wireless Boulevard
Hauppauge, New York 11788

Library of Congress Catalog Card No. 85-15635

International Standard Book No. 0-8120-3523-2

Library of Congress Cataloging-in-Publication Data
Pienciak, Anne.
   J.R.R. Tolkien's Hobbit and Lord of the rings.

   (Barron's book notes)
   Bibliography: p. 131
   Summary: A guide to reading "The Hobbit" and "Lord
of the Rings" with a critical and appreciative mind
encouraging analysis of plot, style, form, and
structure. Also includes background on the author's
life and times, sample tests, term paper suggestions,
and a reading list.
   1. Tolkien, J. R. R. (John Ronald Reuel), 1872–1973—
Criticism and interpretation.   2. Tolkien, J. R. R.
(John Ronald Reuel), 1892–1973. Hobbit.   3. Tolkien,
J. R. R. (John Ronald Reuel), 1892–1973. Lord of the
rings.   4. Fantastic fiction, English—History and
criticism.   1. Tolkien, J.R.R. (John Ronald Reuel),
1892–1973. Hobbit.   2. Tolkien, J.R.R. (John
Ronald Reuel), 1892–1973. Lord of the rings.
3. English literature—History and criticism]
I. Title. II. Series.
PR6039.032Z693 1986   823'.912   85-15635
ISBN 0-8120-3523-2

CONTENTS

ADVISORY BOARD

HOW TO USE THIS BOOK

You have to know how to approach literature in order to get the most out of it. This *Barron's Book Notes* volume follows a plan based on methods used by some of the best students to read a work of literature.

Begin with the guide's section on the author's life and times. As you read, try to form a clear picture of the author's personality, circumstances, and motives for writing the work. This background usually will make it easier for you to hear the author's tone of voice, and follow where the author is heading.

Then go over the rest of the introductory material—such sections as those on the plot, characters, setting, themes, and style of the work. Underline, or write down in your notebook, particular things to watch for, such as contrasts between characters and repeated literary devices. At this point, you may want to develop a system of symbols to use in marking your text as you read. (Of course, you should only mark up a book you own, not one that belongs to another person or a school.) Perhaps you will want to use a different letter for each character's name, a different number for each major theme of the book, a different color for each important symbol or literary device. Be prepared to mark up the pages of your book as you read. Put your marks in the margins so you can find them again easily.

Now comes the moment you've been waiting for— the time to start reading the work of literature. You may want to put aside your *Barron's Book Notes* volume until you've read the work all the way through. Or you may want to alternate, reading the *Book Notes* analysis of each section as soon as you have finished reading the corresponding part of the original. Before you move on, reread crucial passages you don't fully understand. (Don't take this guide's analysis for granted—make up your own mind as to what the work means.)

Once you've finished the whole work of literature, you may want to review it right away, so you can firm up your ideas about what it means. You may want to leaf through the book concentrating on passages you marked in reference to one character or one theme. This is also a good time to reread the *Book Notes* introductory material, which pulls together insights on specific topics.

When it comes time to prepare for a test or to write a paper, you'll already have formed ideas about the work. You'll be able to go back through it, refreshing your memory as to the author's exact words and perspective, so that you can support your opinions with evidence drawn straight from the work. Patterns will emerge, and ideas will fall into place; your essay question or term paper will almost write itself. Give yourself a dry run with one of the sample tests in the guide. These tests present both multiple-choice and essay questions. An accompanying section gives answers to the multiple-choice questions as well as suggestions for writing the essays. If you have to select a term paper topic, you may choose one from the list of suggestions in this book. This guide also provides you with a reading list, to help you when you start research for a term paper, and a selection of provocative comments by critics, to spark your thinking before you write.

THE AUTHOR AND HIS TIMES

When you were younger, did you ever make up stories about the people and places around your home? Maybe there was an abandoned house that in your imagination became haunted by ghosts, or an old neighbor woman that you envisioned as a witch. This fantasizing isn't very different from what many writers do when they transform their experiences into fiction. J. R. R. Tolkien, in his invention of Middle-earth, has done this to a greater degree than most. *The Hobbit* and, even more so, *The Lord of the Rings* were the fruits of a lifetime's work, and Tolkien incorporated into them the landscape of his childhood, his interest in philology (the study of languages), his religious faith, his own vivid imagination, and his attitudes toward the world and the events happening around him.

The first three years of Tolkien's life were spent in South Africa, where he had been born in 1892. His mother returned to England in 1895 with him and his younger brother. His father stayed in South Africa, planning to join the family later, but within a few months he contracted rheumatic fever and died.

The Tolkiens settled in the small English town of Sarehole, where the widow struggled to raise her children alone. As he grew, Tolkien showed an aptitude for language, and under his mother's tutelage studied Latin and French. An avid reader, he especially loved fairy tales. His favorite was the story of Sigurd, the dragon slayer. It wasn't the hero but the dragon Fafnir who intrigued him. The dragon represented a world that was exciting and dangerous, yet that was safely removed from his own life. Tolkien later recalled, ". . . the world that contained even the imagination of Fafnir was richer and more beautiful, at whatever the cost or peril." His fascination with dragons was later to appear in the character Smaug in *The Hobbit*.

Despite their poverty, it was a happy time for the boys, and in later years Tolkien recalled the countryside and its people with great fondness. In fact, the land and the people of Sarehole were to become part of his books, as the Shire and its whimsical inhabitants, the hobbits. You can see elements of his childhood home in hobbit country. The Sarehole mill became an important landmark near Bag End, Bilbo's home, and the miller's evil-looking son was transformed into Ted Sandyman, the unscrupulous hobbit who contributes to the polluting of the Shire in *The Lord of the Rings*. "The Shire," Tolkien once said, "is very like the kind of world in which I first became aware of things." At another time, he said, "I took the idea of the hobbits from the village people and the children."

Tolkien became absorbed in the study of language. After his teachers introduced him to Anglo-Saxon, or Old English, he began to read heroic tales such as *Beowulf* and *Sir Gawain and the Green Knight*. Next he turned to Old Norse and the Norse sagas. On his own, he rummaged through the local bookstore for books on philology and archaic languages. Then he began to invent his own languages and alphabets. He developed complex histories for his languages, earlier words that evolved into later words, just as the Old English "stan" evolved into "stone" in modern English.

Not surprisingly, Tolkien went to Oxford University to study philology. One day he discovered a Finnish grammar book. While the words themselves enthralled him, Tolkien's imagination was also fired by the tales written in this strange language. He delved into Finnish mythology and found himself wishing that there was such a body of work for England. It was perhaps at this point he first thought of writing a mythology himself.

Now Tolkien began work on a new language, based on Finnish—his "mad hobby," as he called it. He felt that the language needed a history to support it: a language can't exist without the people who speak it. Tolkien decided that this language was spoken by a race of elves who had already appeared in the poetry he was writing. This poetry was to form the basis of the vast mythology Tolkien wrote about a land called Middle-earth. Just as his languages were based on actual languages, his mythology incorporated elements of the myths and legends that Tolkien admired.

Around this time, World War I began, and England declared war on Germany. Tolkien entered the British army as an officer. Before going off to war, he married his childhood sweetheart, Edith Bratt. Like Tolkien, whose mother died when he was 12, Edith was an orphan. They had fallen in love when he was 16 and she was 19. Their guardians, however, had found out about the romance and had forbidden the lovers to meet until Tolkien turned 21, when he would legally be an adult. He incorporated this long separation into *The Lord of the Rings,* in the romance between Aragorn and Arwen.

Tolkien was sent to France, where he took part in the 1916 Battle of the Somme, a costly battle for the Allied forces. The slaughter there of thousands of young British soldiers left a lasting impression on Tolkien. In addition, the land had been desolated by trench warfare and the use of heavy artillery. His description of the desolation around Mordor has often been cited for its resemblance to the war-torn landscapes in Europe. Many of his colleagues who had been through the war saw its influence on Tolkien in scenes where he describes not only the horror of war, but also the sense of close comradeship and the quiet joys of little things.

Those who survived the Battle of the Somme faced death from an unexpected quarter in the following months. Influenza and trench fever swept the ranks, affecting soldiers and officers alike. Tolkien contracted a particularly bad case of trench fever and was shipped back to England in late 1916. He spent his long recovery working on his mythology. The war ended in late 1918. Tolkien had survived, only to find that all but one of his close friends had died. To someone who valued friendship so highly, this was a great blow.

Tolkien once said that at the heart of his books is the realization of the inevitability of death. At the age of 24, he had already faced not only the widespread death of the war, but also the personal losses of his parents and friends.

Tolkien slowly returned to academic life. He moved through a series of university positions, culminating in his election to a professorship at Oxford. He published several scholarly works that won respect in his field, including a landmark lecture on *Beowulf,* the famous Old English epic poem.

But he began to feel increasingly alienated from the world about him. Postwar England was rapidly changing with the growth of technology and industry. The way of life he loved so much and had risked his life to defend in war was disappearing. He watched sadly as trees were cut down and countryside was taken over by city, all in the name of progress.

Tolkien's answer was to turn to the myths and heroic legends of the past. He also continued to work on his own mythology. By this time, he had developed several new languages and a complex history and mythology for the races who spoke them. This hobby, as Tolkien modestly called it, was his consuming passion, but he never expected it to arouse much interest in others. He wrote several poems and stories that were published in a university weekly, but there was nothing yet to catch the popular imagination.

That was to change with his invention of hobbits—short, jolly folk with hairy feet and a love of tobacco pipes. One day while sitting at his desk and grading papers, Tolkien came upon a blank page. He wrote on it, "In a hole in the ground there lived a hobbit." Almost ten years after he had written that first line, Tolkien completed *The Hobbit*, the story of a timid hobbit named Bilbo Baggins, who sets out on an adventure with a troop of dwarves and a wizard. Tolkien incorporated into his book elements from his mythology, including the dwarves and elves. His childhood memories and the inventive imagination that so delighted his own children gave the book its droll humor and its main character, Bilbo. In the hobbit, Tolkien had found a character his readers could identify with and follow into the heroic world of myth and legends.

The Hobbit was published in 1937 as a children's book. It was met with great enthusiasm and received several awards, including the prestigious *New York Herald Tribune* prize as the year's best children's book. At the request of his publishers, Tolkien set out to write a sequel to *The Hobbit*. The publishers had wanted another children's book, but it soon became apparent that the new book was taking on a more profound meaning and would far surpass *The Hobbit* in depth as well as length.

When Tolkien at last submitted his new novel, *The Lord of the Rings*, his publisher thought that it was a work of genius but that it would probably be a commercial flop. However, when the first book of the trilogy, *The Fellowship of the Ring*, was published in 1954, it had respectable sales that quickly increased to a phenomenal rate. The other books of the trilogy, *The Two Towers* and *The Return of the King*, were published sooner than planned because of the popular demand.

The critics offered a range of comment on Tolkien. Some gave him great reviews, and he was awarded a prize for the best fantasy novel of 1956. Others sharpened their pencils and attacked the trilogy mercilessly. They said it was badly written, and dismissed it as escapist fantasy. According to these critics, Tolkien's popularity would quickly fade. But such negative prophecies proved wrong.

Tolkien's books soon developed a wide following, especially on college campuses in the United States. In the 1960s, Tolkien's message of love and peace and respect for nature appealed to students looking for new meaning in their lives. Clubs were formed and fan magazines were published for the sole purpose of discussing his books.

Tolkien, meanwhile, had retired from teaching in 1958. He published several more small works of fiction. But most of his effort went into his mythology, which he still had hopes of publishing. The task was a huge one. Tolkien had an assortment of manuscripts to work with, some dating back to his college days. Through the years, he had written conflicting versions of some stories from his mythology and had left others unfinished. The inconsistencies had to be ironed out and the gaps filled in. Facts also had to be corrected where they disagreed with *The Hobbit* and *The Lord of the Rings*. This work remained unfinished at his death in 1973.

The job of finishing the book was taken on by his son Christopher, who edited the manuscripts and compiled a coherent history of Middle-earth, from its creation through to the events recounted in *The Lord of the Rings*. In 1977 this history was published as *The Silmarillion*. If you read it, you will find the book very different from Tolkien's novels. It contains a great deal of legends and tales, some more fully outlined than others, but none with the plot and character development typical of a story. (In this way, *The Silmarillion* is even more like the ancient epics than Tolkien's other books.) If you want to know more about Middle-earth, however, the book contains a wealth of information about the land and races created by Tolkien's fertile imagination.

THE NOVELS

The Plots

THE HOBBIT

Bilbo Baggins is a hobbit, one of a race of short, timid creatures who live in cozy tunnels and who prefer to keep their lives ordered and predictable. One day, he unexpectedly finds himself playing host to Gandalf the wizard and thirteen dwarves. The dwarves, with Gandalf's help, plan to travel to the Lonely Mountain to recover the treasure that a dragon named Smaug stole from their people long ago. Gandalf has selected Bilbo to be their burglar. The dwarves aren't too happy with the wizard's choice, especially when Bilbo faints at the first talk of danger. But Gandalf insists there is more to the little hobbit than meets the eye.

Bilbo himself isn't sure that he's happy about being chosen burglar. But a part of him does yearn for adventure, and so one spring morning he finds himself setting out for Lonely Mountain with Gandalf and the thirteen dwarves. He doesn't prove very helpful at first. But then something happens that changes Bilbo's life. He finds a magic ring that makes him invisible, and has several opportunities to use it to rescue the dwarves from danger and imprisonment. They become quite impressed by him, and even rely on him, just as Gandalf foretold.

Bilbo and the dwarves finally reach Lonely Mountain, the home of Smaug the dragon. The dwarves send Bilbo down a secret passage to the dragon's lair. Bilbo has more confidence in himself now and not only steals a cup, but manages to hold his own in a conversation with the wily Smaug—not an easy thing to do.

Furious that someone has dared steal a piece of his treasure, Smaug attacks the mountainside where the dwarves have their camp. Then he flies toward Lake-town, to punish the inhabitants for helping the dwarves.

The people of Lake-town run at the sight of Smaug, but one man, Bard, holds his ground. He kills the dragon with his last arrow and escapes before Smaug falls, smashing the town. Believing the dwarves are dead, an army of men, led by Bard, and an army of elves march toward the Lonely Mountain to divide the treasure. They find to their surprise that the dwarves are still alive.

Bard, because he killed the dragon, claims his rightful share of the treasure. When the dwarves refuse to surrender it, the army besieges the mountain. Bilbo tries to end the dispute by stealing the Arkenstone, the piece of treasure most valued by the leader of the dwarves. He gives the jewel to Bard, hoping it can be used to force the dwarves to negotiate. Bilbo's bravery wins him praise from all but the dwarves, who are furious with him. When more dwarves arrive from the north, they are determined to fight.

Just as war begins to break out, an army of goblins and wild wolves attack. The dwarves, elves, and men forget their differences and join together to keep from being killed. Help comes in the nick of time, and the goblins are defeated.

Bilbo finds that he's a hero, honored by men and

elves and even given a share of the treasure. But he's had enough of adventure and sets off for home with Gandalf. Once there, he finds that his house and furnishings are being auctioned off, since everyone believed him dead. Finally, everything is straightened out and he's able to settle down again into his old, comfortable life. Although from then on, he's considered eccentric by his neighbors, he continues his friendship with elves and dwarves and the wizard, happily recounting his tales to any who will listen.

THE LORD OF THE RINGS

Long after the events in *The Hobbit*, Bilbo again leaves the Shire, but not before reluctantly passing on his magic ring to his heir, Frodo Baggins.

Many years later, Frodo learns from Gandalf, the wizard, that his ring is *the* Ring, which belonged to the evil ruler Sauron. Sauron was thought to have been destroyed ages ago. But now he has reappeared in his ancient stronghold of Mordor. His Ring was presumed lost, but Sauron has discovered that it's presently in the hands of a hobbit named Baggins, who lives in the Shire.

To protect the inhabitants of the Shire from Sauron's wrath, Frodo decides to take the Ring and leave Bag End for Rivendell with three friends—Merry, Pippin, and Sam. Gandalf was supposed to accompany them, but no word has been heard from him. On the way, the four hobbits are closely pursued by menacing Black Riders, servants of Sauron. The hobbits are unprepared for the dangers that face them, and several times they're almost killed because of their foolishness. Fortunately, they are joined by a strange, secretive man called Strider, who offers to lead them to Rivendell.

One night, Frodo is wounded in an attack by the Black Riders. His friends bring him to Rivendell, where he is cured by Elrond, the leader of the Half-elven (a race of people who are half elf and half human).

A council meets in Rivendell to decide what to do about the Ring. It's agreed the Ring must be destroyed, for the temptation to use it is too strong, and anyone who does use it will be corrupted by its power. Frodo takes on the task of bringing the Ring to Mordor and casting it into the volcano where it was forged.

Strider takes this opportunity to reveal his true name: Aragorn. He is rightful heir to the throne of Gondor, which has been ruled by stewards for many years in the absence of a king. He plans to return to Gondor, to aid in its fight against Sauron and to claim his crown.

When Frodo departs from Rivendell, he is accompanied by representatives of all the free races of Middle-earth: Gandalf the wizard, Legolas the elf, Gimli the dwarf, Aragorn and Boromir of the race of men, and Frodo's hobbit friends, Sam, Merry, and Pippin. While passing through the mines of Moria, the company is threatened by a Balrog, a terrifying creature of flame and shadow. While fighting the Balrog, Gandalf and the creature plunge into a deep abyss and are both thought killed.

The rest of the company splits up further south. Boromir has fallen under the influence of the Ring and tries to take it from Frodo. Frodo runs away and decides to travel on to Mordor alone, but his faithful servant, Sam, insists on going with him.

Meanwhile, the others are attacked by orcs, an evil race created by Sauron. (Goblins and orcs are the same thing—Tolkien changed the name in *The Lord of the Rings*.) Merry and Pippin are captured, and Boromir dies defending the hobbits. After giving Boromir a hero's funeral, Aragorn, Legolas, and Gimli follow the trail of the orcs, hoping to rescue their friends. Instead, they find Gandalf, who has survived his fight with the Balrog and has emerged with renewed power. Gandalf tells the others that Merry and Pippin are safe: they escaped the orcs and are now with the Ents of Fangorn Forest. The Ents, who are shepherds of the trees, have been roused by the hobbits' story to attack Saruman, an evil wizard in league with Sauron.

Gandalf, Legolas, Aragorn, and Gimli enlist the men of Rohan, whose country is threatened by Saruman's growing power, to join the fight against the wizard. With the help of the Ents, Saruman is overthrown.

Frodo and Sam, meanwhile, begin their long journey toward Mordor. They are followed by Gollum, the miserable creature who owned the Ring before Bilbo found it. Frodo and Sam capture him and make him promise to help them. Gollum guides them to a secret passage into Mordor. But in doing so, he also treacherously leads them into a trap. The secret passage he takes them through is the lair of a giant spider named Shelob, who he hopes will kill them so he can recover the Ring.

Shelob attacks Frodo, paralyzing him with her sting. Thinking that Frodo is dead, Sam charges the spider and succeeds in driving her off. Then he takes the Ring, intending to carry on the quest. Before he can leave, however, some orcs find Frodo's body and carry it into their fortress. Sam overhears them say that Frodo isn't dead, but only poisoned. Then the gates of the tower close behind the orcs, and Sam finds himself locked out.

Meanwhile, the others fight desperately to save Minas Tirith, the capital of Gondor, from Sauron's army. Against great odds, they win. Aragorn proves his claim to kingship by his great healing power: it is said that the hands of a king are the hands of a healer. But he doesn't yet claim the throne. First he leads what remains of the army to the gates of Mordor. Against Sauron's might they seem pitifully weak. Their only hope is to distract Sauron while Frodo and Sam travel through Mordor and destroy the Ring. If Frodo succeeds, Sauron will fall. If Frodo fails, they will all die or be enslaved.

Inside Mordor, Sam has managed to rescue Frodo from Sauron's orcs. The two hobbits creep through the desolate landscape of Mordor. Frodo grows so weak from resisting the power of the Ring that he can barely crawl, and Sam carries him for a while. When they at last reach the Crack of Doom where the Ring is to be destroyed, Frodo's will snaps, and he claims the Ring as his own. But Gollum appears and fights him for the Ring, biting it off Frodo's hand. Still gloating, Gollum falls into the flames and is destroyed along with the Ring. With the Ring destroyed, Sauron is vanquished forever. Frodo and Sam are rescued from the ruins of Mordor by eagles, and together with Aragorn's army, they return to Minas Tirith in triumph.

There is much feasting and rejoicing as Aragorn is declared king and marries Arwen, the daughter of Elrond. The hobbits have all become heroes. But now they are ready to go home, and they head for the Shire. When they get back, however, they find that things have changed. Saruman has gained control, along with his ruffians, and is bullying the hobbits and destroying the beautiful countryside of the Shire. But Frodo, Sam, Merry, and Pippin have learned much from their adventures and quickly set things right.

All seems well, until Frodo falls sick. He has been wounded too many times—by the Black Rider's knife, by the Ring, and by Gollum. It is ironical that even though he saved the Shire, he cannot enjoy it anymore. One autumn day he sets sail with Bilbo and Gandalf across the sea to the Blessed Realm, where he may at last find peace.

The Characters

The following are major characters in *The Hobbit* and in *The Lord of the Rings*.

THE HOBBIT

Bilbo Baggins

Bilbo is the small, timid hero of *The Hobbit*. It has been pointed out by some readers that in his thoughts and actions he is representative of modern man. Thus, adults are able to identify with him and not feel so out of place in Tolkien's heroic world of wizards and dwarves. Bilbo is also, fittingly, a character that children can readily identify with, since *The Hobbit* was written as a children's story and today is considered by many to be a classic in that genre.

Bilbo can also be seen as an example of Everyman, reflecting the potential greatness in us all. He's just an ordinary person. And with his small stature and simple, timid nature, he's certainly an unlikely hero.

Yet, despite his apparent weaknesses, Bilbo finds the strength to become heroic. His strength seems to come from the things he holds dear—frequent meals, a peaceful ordered life, and his pipe—the very things that, to some, make him seem so ordinary and laughable. And at the end of the book, these things are still important to Bilbo, a sign that these are qualities Tolkien wanted to emphasize. The only way Bilbo has changed is that he has become more self-confident, more capable of taking care of himself and of others.

But is Bilbo really an example of Everyman? In some ways he's *not* your average hobbit. For one thing, he's a bachelor, and a wealthy one at that. For another, his mother was from the Took family, hobbits with a tendency to be more daring and adventurous than most. This leads some readers to say that Bilbo is a member of an elite group, a select few who are superior to the common people. You'll have to decide for yourself what Tolkien intended—whether Bilbo represents the potential for greatness in even the weakest individual, or whether Bilbo is part of an elite circle that most people can never reach.

Gandalf

Gandalf is the wizard who assists Bilbo and the dwarves on their journey. Like a typical wizard,

Gandalf appears as an old man dressed in blue robes and a tall pointed hat. Wizards are skilled in magic, and Gandalf's specialty is fire. In the beginning of *The Hobbit*, Bilbo enthusiastically recalls Gandalf's marvelous fireworks. Later in the story, Gandalf puts his skills to more practical use—for example, when he throws the evil wargs into an uproar with a magical fire that clings to their fur.

Wizards are often known for their shrewdness as well as for their magic, and Gandalf is no exception. He defeats the trolls not by magic but by cleverly distracting them until the sun rises and turns them to stone.

Despite his wisdom and magical powers, however, Gandalf can also be seen as a humorous figure. When Gandalf first meets Bilbo, Tolkien describes him in comic terms as having long, bushy eyebrows that stick out beyond his hat. He can be childish at times, acting grumpy in a rainstorm, or vexed that Elrond is the first to find the secret letters on Thorin's map.

Bilbo remembers from his childhood the wizard's fabulous fireworks, wonderful gadgets, and thrilling stories of adventure. Just as Fafnir the dragon excited the imagination of the young Tolkien, so Gandalf intrigues Bilbo with a dangerous world, far removed from the hobbit's comfortable life. As the story of *The Hobbit* begins, Gandalf reenters Bilbo's life and starts the hobbit on an adventure into that dangerous world.

Thorin Oakenshield

Thorin is the self-important leader of the dwarves and the grandson of Thrain, the last king under Lonely Mountain. The most completely developed character of the thirteen dwarves, he shows both the weaknesses and the strengths of his race. Accordingly, readers may find him ambiguous. He can be petty, selfish, and pompous, but he can also be heroic and awe-inspiring. He's motivated at first by greed and the desire for revenge, but when he reaches Lonely Mountain he begins to feel a higher purpose, claiming his rightful title as king under the mountain. He succumbs to a weakness of his race—possessiveness—but later redeems himself through courage in battle.

Gollum

Gollum was once a hobbitlike creature, but when Bilbo meets him he has degenerated both morally and physically. Gollum has become a "small, slimy creature" with long webby feet, who lives in the heart of the mountain, paddling his boat on a subterranean lake. His most prized possession is his ring, which can make him invisible. He's obsessed with this ring, calling it by the name he uses for himself: "my precious."

Gollum's moral degeneration can be seen in his deceitful actions toward Bilbo. Yet Tolkien also depicts Gollum as a lonely, pitiable creature, who weeps at the loss of his one precious possession.

Bard

When Bard first appears in the story, he is just an anonymous inhabitant of Lake-town. He proves his worth when he arouses the town to face the dragon Smaug's attack, and succeeds in killing Smaug when everyone else has given up the fight.

Bard is a heroic figure, a grim leader of strength and discipline, who serves as a contrast to Bilbo, the timid hobbit. Yet they both become heroes because of their determination to do what must be done, regardless of the consequences. Ironically, Bard's name is an old word for a certain type of poet who in England and Ireland's past often composed tales of heroism. When you read the book, try to decide whether this is a joke on Tolkien's part or whether in some ways Bard is more like a poet than a warrior.

Smaug

Dragons are often depicted in legends as jealously guarding a great treasure. Tolkien stays true to this tradition in his portrayal of Smaug, who long ago drove the dwarves from their home in the Lonely Mountain and now jealously broods over treasure stolen from them and others. Dragons also have a reputation as wily talkers, and Smaug ranks with the best of them. He never says what he means, and even his polite words carry veiled menace. He skillfully plays on Bilbo's doubts and seeks to trick him into giving himself away.

Folklore describes dragons as misers who have been transformed by their greed. Dragons have also long been a symbol for the lure of gold and the evil that wealth brings. Tolkien uses this association between dragons and greed. He even refers to the corrupting effect of the treasure as "dragon-sickness."

The Master

The Master, the greedy and scheming leader of Lake-town, seems in some ways a human counterpart to the dragon Smaug. He, too, is a wily talker, carefully choosing his words to manipulate others. He succumbs to the dragon-sickness—greed—and steals the share of the treasure that was to go to Lake-town.

The Master contrasts with Bard, who always says exactly what he thinks, even if others don't want to hear it. Also unlike Bard, the Master turns his back on his town, thinking only to save his own skin. In his selfishness he proves himself to be a poor leader.

THE LORD OF THE RINGS

Frodo Baggins

The hero of *The Lord of the Rings* trilogy, Frodo is Bilbo's young cousin. He inherits Bilbo's home and his magic ring when Bilbo leaves the Shire. Frodo's adventure begins when he learns that the ring is actually a thing of great evil. It is *the* Ring, made by Sauron, the Dark Lord, who is now trying to regain it. Frodo sets off on what will become a long and dangerous quest to destroy the Ring.

Readers often compare the characters of Bilbo and Frodo. Like Bilbo, Frodo is a bachelor and has some eccentric blood; his mother was a Brandy-buck, a family of adventurous hobbits like the Tooks. Also like Bilbo, he starts out as a somewhat foolish hobbit and through his travels matures into a heroic figure.

But there are important differences between the two hobbits. Frodo is not the comic character that Bilbo was. He has benefited from Bilbo's knowledge, learning the lore and language of the elves and thereby earning their respect. His quest is more selfless than Bilbo's. He doesn't seek to win a treasure, but hopes to destroy one (the Ring of

Sauron) for the good of all Middle-earth. Unlike Bilbo, Frodo can't use the Ring to help him with his task. And, finally, his story is in the end tragic—while he saves Middle-earth from destruction, he can no longer enjoy its beauties. He suffers too greatly from his wounds and from the loss of the Ring. His departure for the Blessed Realm at the end of the book is interpreted by some readers to be a symbolic death and also bears some similarity to the departure of the legendary King Arthur to Avalon, a magical island.

Frodo is sometimes considered a Christ-figure, because he undergoes great suffering for the sake of others (Tolkien himself would not say if this is what he intended. He wanted readers to make their own interpretation.) While he becomes weaker physically through the course of his trials, he also becomes stronger spiritually. A certain light seems to shine within Frodo, reminiscent of the description of saints. When Frodo leaves Middle-earth in the company of Gandalf, Galadriel, and other beings of great power, this increases the sense that Frodo has become something more than human.

Aragorn (Strider, the Dúnadan, Elessar the Elf-Stone)

As Strider, chief of the Rangers who secretly guard the Shire, Aragorn guides Frodo and his friends to the safety of Rivendell. There Aragorn reveals that he's the descendant of kings. Through the rest of the book, Aragorn must prove himself worthy of the throne of Gondor.

Some readers feel that Aragorn should be considered as a second hero of *The Lord of the Rings* who is equally as important as Frodo. As you read, note the contrasts and parallels between the two characters. Aragorn's quest is to regain his inheritance, the throne of Gondor, whereas Frodo's quest is to destroy his inheritance (the Ring given him by Bilbo). Aragorn is a man of heroic stature and his tasks are those of war and leadership, whereas Frodo's are more spiritual: he must resist the temptation of the Ring.

Like Frodo, Aragorn continues to grow in character through the course of the book. In the beginning, he's shown as a loner, unaccustomed to friendship. At first glance he even seems disreputable, and the hobbits are suspicious of him. In Rivendell, he reveals that as rightful heir to the throne of Gondor, he plans to go there to present his claim. But when the loss of Gandalf forces him to take over leadership of the group of hobbits, he can no longer think only of his personal interests.

Aragorn is a very private man, yet Tolkien reveals glimpses of strong emotions: resentment at the simple folk who scorn him, not knowing that he protects them from great danger; loneliness at living the life of an outcast; and deep love for Arwen, Elrond's daughter.

The romance between Arwen and Aragorn is only hinted at in the book, and their marriage at the end of the story may come as a surprise to you. In an appendix of *The Lord of the Rings*, you will find the full story of their romance.

Sam Gamgee (Samwise)

Sam Gamgee, the son of Frodo's gardener, sets out with Frodo on the quest to destroy the Ring. He proves himself a faithful servant.

Tolkien once said that Sam was modeled on the

noncommissioned soldiers he served with in World War I. Tolkien had found the common soldiers much more likable than his fellow commissioned officers. Years later he said, "My 'Sam Gamgee' is indeed a reflection of the English soldier, of the privates and batmen [soldiers who perform various services for superior officers] I knew in the 1914 war, and recognized as so far superior to myself."

Because he's just a gardener's son, Sam serves as the best example of Tolkien's theme about the greatness in common people. Sam at times seems simpleminded and shows a lack of understanding of the true seriousness of a situation. But his name, Samwise, hints that he's not so foolish as he seems. Sometimes he can be very perceptive in determining the motives of others. His greatest virtue is loyalty. Because of his devotion to Frodo, he too becomes a hero. It is Sam who rescues Frodo from the orcs and helps Frodo in his painful journey through Mordor, even carrying him when Frodo is too weak to crawl.

Some readers view Sam as a negative stereotype of a member of the working class. They object to what they see as his simplemindedness and his doglike devotion to Frodo. They feel that Sam should be an equal to Frodo. What do you think of the relationship between Sam and Frodo? Is it possible or desirable in the world today?

Gollum (Sméagol)

Gollum, the miserable creature who owned the Ring before Bilbo, reappears in *The Lord of the Rings*. He reveals the location of the Ring to Sauron, who sends the Black Riders to the Shire after Frodo.

Much later in the trilogy, Gollum guides Frodo into Mordor and betrays him by leading him into the lair of Shelob the spider. Even so, neither Frodo nor Sam can bring himself to kill Gollum. Their mercy is rewarded, for Gollum brings about his own destruction as well as the destruction of the Ring.

Many people think of Gollum as Frodo's doppelgänger, or alter ego. A doppelgänger is a character who is strongly connected to the main character, and who seems to represent a hidden facet, often the darker side, of the main character's personality. While doppelgängers are used as a literary device, they also appear often in folklore. Gollum's connection to Frodo is through the Ring. They have both possessed the Ring, though Gollum uses it selfishly for evil purposes, while Frodo unwillingly accepts it in order to destroy it. Frodo, unlike the other characters, can understand Gollum's obsession with the Ring and the misery it has caused him, for Gollum represents what may happen to Frodo if he succumbs to the Ring's power. In Frodo, Gollum sees what he might have been, had it not been for the Ring. Gollum's grief at the loss of the Ring foreshadows Frodo's own pain and unhappiness after the Ring is gone. In the end, like most doppelgängers, Gollum is finally destroyed, representing the destruction of the evil that Frodo has had to struggle with in himself.

Some people see Gollum as a tragic figure. He has not been completely corrupted by the Ring. A part of him remembers his old life, and by implication, he can then still remember and comprehend good, something that characters such as Sauron, who are totally evil, cannot. Because part of his old self remains, he's tormented. He both hates the Ring and craves it desperately. The conflict between his two sides is revealed as he alternates between his original hobbitlike personality (Sméagol), speaking normally and eager to please, and his Gollum side, nasty and treacherous. But Gollum seems doomed from the beginning, for his destiny, as has been hinted throughout the trilogy, is to be destroyed with the Ring.

Do you sympathize with Gollum? Why or why not? Do you think he deserves his fate?

Gandalf (Mithrandir, the Grey Pilgrim, the White Rider)

Gandalf the Grey is one of three wizards who appear in *The Lord of the Rings*. The other two are Saruman the White and Radagast the Brown. Gandalf seems to be a more dignified character in *The Lord of the Rings* than he was in *The Hobbit*. In Rivendell he is revealed as an imposing figure of great power that he uses for unselfish purposes. He says that he's a steward over all living things, and he works to protect them from evil.

Whereas Saruman is tempted to use his power to further his own ends, Gandalf is content to help others in their struggles against evil, placing himself in the service of all who need him. This is viewed by some readers as a Christian image and they interpret Gandalf as being saintlike. (It should be pointed out that such selflessness is considered a virtue by many religions, and also by many nonreligious people. It need not be interpreted as a Christian idea.) Like Frodo, Gandalf sacrifices himself for the sake of others, apparently dying in his fight with the Balrog, and later being resurrected.

Tolkien once said that Gandalf is an angel. But it is not clear if he meant it literally, or meant only that Gandalf was similar to an angel, someone with great power who is sent as a guardian.

Some people argue that Gandalf is the true hero of the book. He has been opposing Sauron for ages, whereas others such as Frodo and Aragorn appear only near the end of the long battle against evil. Throughout the story, Gandalf works behind the scenes, guiding the others and making it possible for them to fulfill their roles in the struggle. When the ring is destroyed, Gandalf's long guardianship of Middle-earth is at last over. With Frodo, he passes over the sea to the Blessed Realm.

Gandalf can be compared to Merlin the magician, who appears in Arthurian legend. Like Gandalf, Merlin doesn't use his powers to further his own ends, but instead acts for the good of England, which is threatened with internal conflict and with conquest by foreigners. He acts as a councilor, sometimes using his magic to help things along, but never using it in any outright attempt to force events to follow his will. Gandalf's relationship with Aragorn is comparable to Merlin's relationship with Arthur, whom Merlin helps to win the throne of England and establish a lasting peace.

Sauron

Sauron, the Dark Lord of Mordor, is the personification of evil in *The Lord of the Rings*. He is also referred to as the Necromancer in *The Hobbit*. Tolkien's only physical description of him is as a lidless red eye. This serves to heighten the sense of dread surrounding him, more than any other description could. Through Sauron, Tolkien offers his own ideas about evil: that nothing started out evil, that evil cannot create but can only pervert, that evil cannot comprehend good and so cannot predict the actions of good, and that evil destroys free will. Through the power of the Ring, Sauron intends to enslave the inhabitants of Middle-earth.

Saruman (Sharkey)

Saruman the White is a wizard like Gandalf and is head of the White Council that originally drove Sauron (the Necromancer) from Mirkwood Forest. But Saruman has studied the ways of the enemy and has fallen into the temptation to be like him, to rule the world as he sees fit. When he speaks to Gandalf of the need to drop weaker allies, and when he defends murder if it's committed for greater good, he may remind you of some modern political speakers who believe that anything can be justified by an appeal to some nebulous greater good. That, coupled with his destructive technology, makes him a very modern villain, a little more recognizable than Sauron. Saruman, like all of Tolkien's totally evil characters, cannot understand good and hates those who are good. For example, he doesn't understand Frodo's mercy toward him near the end of the trilogy, and he hates Frodo for it.

Some readers see Saruman as Gandalf's alter ego, in much the same way that Gollum is Frodo's alter ego. Saruman had the potential to be what Gandalf is, a wise and powerful being. Likewise, Gandalf has the potential to become like Saruman, for he has the same abilities and is faced with the same temptations as his fallen counterpart.

Merry and Pippin (Meriadoc Brandybuck and Peregrine Took)

These two hobbits, friends of Frodo, serve as a balance to Frodo and Sam. Even more so than Sam and Frodo, they are foolish, innocent, and unprepared for the trials ahead. Where Sam and Frodo face mainly mental trials, Merry and Pippin endure the physical trials of war. It is through their eyes that you see most of the action in Rohan and Gondor. And they both come face to face with evil, when Pippin is questioned by Sauron through the *palantír*, the stone of seeing, and when Merry meets the leader of the Black Riders in battle. They emerge from their trials stronger and wiser, and able to defend their own home. As an outward sign of this internal change, they have also grown taller.

Boromir and Faramir

Boromir and Faramir are both sons of Denethor, the steward of Gondor. You first meet Boromir in Book II, where he joins the company who set out from Rivendell with Frodo. Faramir doesn't appear until Book IV, when Frodo and Sam meet him in Ithilien, just outside the borders of Mordor. Faramir is the leader of a band of men from Gondor who are engaged in guerrilla warfare, harassing Sauron's armies.

Boromir and Faramir serve to contrast the warrior with the spiritual man. Boromir is characterized by his brother as closer to the "middle" race of men, the warriors. He is a proud man, who loves fighting, glory, and power. He falls under the temptation of the Ring, for he believes that force can be used in the fight for good. Faramir, on the other hand, is of the "high" race, which is more noble than the middle race in Tolkien's scheme of things. A lover of knowledge, he hates war and fights only to protect the land he loves. He easily resists the temptation of the Ring, for he recognizes the danger of power over others.

Théoden and Denethor

Théoden, king of Rohan, is a warrior of the middle race of men, while Denethor, steward of Gondor, is of the high race, a lover of knowledge. Yet in this case the comparison between "middle" and "high" is reversed, with the warrior appearing in the more favorable light. Théoden believes in the heroic ethic of the Anglo-Saxon epics: "Will shall be the sterner, heart the bolder, spirit the greater as our strength lessens." No matter how the battle goes, he never gives into despair, and eventually dies, fighting to the end. Denethor, on the other hand, prides himself as a man of knowledge. When his knowledge leads him to believe the fight is hopeless, he can't accept defeat and, giving in to despair, commits suicide. Ironically, his suicide indirectly causes Théoden's death.

Éowyn

The niece of Théoden, Éowyn is the most fully developed female character in Tolkien's works. She feels caged, first at having to take care of her ailing uncle, then at being left behind when the army rides into battle. She desires glory, not just dull duty. She falls in love with Aragorn, and when he doesn't return her love, she seeks death in battle. Calling herself Dernhelm, she disguises herself as a young warrior and becomes a hero by killing the leader of the ringwraiths. Éowyn is finally cured of her death wish when she falls in love with Faramir. Instead of earning glory in battle, she now wants to be a healer.

The Ringwraiths (Black Riders, Nazgûl, the Nine, Fell Riders)

Their captain is called the Black Captain, the Dark Captain, the Morgul king, and the Witch-lord of Angmar. The ringwraiths were nine men who served Sauron and fell under the power of the rings he had made for the race of men. Now they have faded into a shadow world and are invisible. Their cry drives men to despair. Some readers say that the ringwraiths couldn't cause such despair unless they themselves felt it.

Tom Bombadil

Tom Bombadil was named after a doll that belonged to Tolkien's daughter. Frodo and his friends meet him when he comes to their rescue in the Old Forest. His appearance is humorous: he is a short old man with yellow boots and a blue coat, and when the hobbits first see him he is hopping and dancing down the path, carrying lilies and singing nonsense songs.

But Tom proves to be a very powerful being. Even the Ring has no effect on him; in fact, he's able to make the Ring vanish. His wife, Goldberry, says that Tom is the Eldest, and master over all. With his great power, he could serve as a strong ally against Sauron. But when Gandalf speaks about him later, he says that Tom is not involved in this battle. The Ring means nothing to Tom, and if they asked him to guard it he would probably forget about it and lose it.

Tom is one of Tolkien's characters who are closely associated with the natural world. In fact, many readers think of Tom Bombadil as a personification of nature. His lack of involvement in the war against Sauron is seen as a sign of nature's neutrality in the war between good and evil.

Treebeard (Fangorn)

Treebeard the Ent is another character who is closely associated with nature. There's a story that Tolkien invented the Ents for one of his sons, who was distressed to see so many trees cut down in the name of progress, and wanted to see the trees get revenge. Treebeard leads the Ents, a race of tree-like creatures, against Saruman, whose orcs have been wantonly cutting down trees.

Like Tom Bombadil, Treebeard is neutral in the war against Sauron. He tells Merry and Pippin that the only reason the Ents attack Saruman is that he has been destroying the forest.

Other Elements

SETTING

The events in *The Hobbit* and *The Lord of the Rings* take place in the imaginary world of Middle-earth, which is inhabited by fantastic people and animals, such as elves, wizards, and dragons, who are rather human in many ways. Some people say that since the works are set in a world that could never exist, they have no relevance to our own. However, many authors have used invented settings to make telling points about the real world. Some well-known examples are *Gulliver's Travels* by Jonathan Swift and *Animal Farm* by George Orwell. Furthermore, according to Tolkien, Middle-earth is nothing more than our own world in the remote past. The name Middle-earth itself is actually an archaic word for the earth. Although wizards, elves, and dragons may no longer exist, the principles ruling Middle-earth are still in effect today.

Tolkien tries to draw you into his fictional world by creating the impression that Middle-earth *is* a real place. He describes in detail the landscape, filling it with the familiar plants and animals of Earth. The books, on one level, are a tour through Middle-earth. You learn the names and background of different landmarks. You also meet the inhabitants of Middle-earth and learn something about their customs and histories. You'll probably enjoy these details, even though most are not essential to the plot. But all this information can also be confusing. In the index at the end of *The Lord of the Rings* you will find the names of people, places, and things. At the beginning of each volume you will find maps to help you follow the action through Middle-earth. Also, a brief history of Middle-earth is given in the end of this guide.

The setting forms a very important part of the story. Places such as the Shire, Rivendell, and Lórien are different forms of utopias, presenting some of Tolkien's thoughts about the ideal society—for example, that humans should live in harmony with nature. Evil is often associated with particular locations, such as Sauron's stronghold in Mordor. It is also associated with mountains and barren landscapes; compare the Desolation of Smaug, for example, with the wastelands around Mordor.

Encounters with danger in Tolkien's books often occur in mountains or in a forest. A character's passage into an underground place or into a dense forest can be interpreted as a descent into the person's subconscious. In other words, the danger that the character faces is symbolic of an internal struggle. So, for example, when Bilbo meets Gollum in the underground lake, he's actually meeting a part of his subconscious. In other words, the episode with Gollum may be interpreted as Bilbo confronting the potential for evil within himself. Tolkien disliked such interpretations, however, and insisted that his books be taken at face value.

THEMES

The following are themes of *The Hobbit* and *The Lord of the Rings*.

1. STRUGGLE BETWEEN GOOD AND EVIL

The forces of good in Middle-earth are engaged in a continuing struggle against evil. What will be the final outcome of this struggle? Some readers think Tolkien indicates evil will prevail, while others say he's optimistic about the ultimate victory of good.

Those feeling Tolkien thinks evil will win out note that it's left to seemingly powerless individuals like Frodo to face the overwhelming force of evil. These individuals must struggle on with no hope for assistance from someone more powerful, and with little hope for victory or even survival. Victory, when it is achieved, comes only at great cost to the forces of good. And it seems to win

only a breathing space, barely enough time to recover before evil again arises and threatens the
freedom of Middle-earth.

Other readers see a strong vein of optimism in
Tolkien's works. They point to the fact that the
inhabitants of Middle-earth are helped in their fight
by a benevolent power. The workings of that power
are seldom visible to the individuals in the midst
of the action, but a larger viewpoint reveals a grand
design. Even evil deeds are turned to good purpose—for example, when Merry and Pippin's capture by the orcs serves to bring them to Fangorn
in time to rouse the Ents against the evil wizard
Saruman. This seems to imply that good is stronger
and more lasting than evil.

Keep these two viewpoints in mind as you read
the book. Look for evidence to support one or the
other, and decide which you think better explains
Tolkien's works.

2. DETERMINISM VS. FREE WILL

The question of determinism is only hinted at in
the last chapter of *The Hobbit*, when Gandalf suggests to Bilbo that his adventures may have been
managed for some higher purpose. But in *The Lord
of the Rings* it is repeatedly emphasized that seemingly random events are part of some grand design. Each of Tolkien's characters there has a big
or small part to play in that design. The actions of
evil characters are turned to good, against their
will. The main weapon of evil—despair—is used
to turn people from their assigned tasks and so foil
the designs of good. These elements in the works
make people seem like puppets manipulated by
opposing powers of good and evil.

Tolkien, however, also notes the importance of free will. His characters are free to accept or reject possible courses of action. The forces of good in *The Lord of the Rings*, such as Gandalf and Galadriel, respect this freedom to choose. They continually tell others that they not only can but must make their own decisions. Not even the prospect of total defeat can justify interfering with the free will of others. The forces of evil, on the other hand, seek to destroy free will.

It may be argued that, according to Tolkien, free will is only an illusion. Many times characters make important decisions without knowing why they made them. Bilbo, for example, is never sure just how he ended up leaving his comfortable home to join the dwarves on their adventure. Do you think that such decisions are truly free, or are Tolkien's characters being manipulated without their knowledge? Keep this question in mind as you read the works.

3. NATURE OF HEROISM

It is in their darkest moments that Tolkien's characters seem to rise above themselves and become truly heroic. Their heroism does not come from great strength or cunning, but from the indomitable will to continue as long as there is a means to resist. This is a kind of heroism that even the physically weak can achieve, as shown by Tolkien's hobbits.

4. RESPONSIBLE USE OF POWER

In Middle-earth, power is a dangerous thing that can turn against those who wield it. The forces of good in Middle-earth, such as Elrond and Gandalf, recognize this danger and are very careful how they use their power. They know that no matter how good their intention, they will find their purpose perverted if they resort to force. The best example of this is their refusal to use the Ring. The Ring gives the power to dominate others, and with it they could overthrow Sauron. But the Ring also dominates the will of whoever wears it. Even if Gandalf used the Ring only out of the worthy desire to help others, he'd fall under its influence and turn into another Dark Lord like Sauron.

Although the forces of good will not use the power to dominate others, they do have other powers available to them—the power to heal, the power to understand, and the power to create beauty. But these seem pitifully small in the face of Sauron's power, and the temptation to "fight fire with fire" is strong.

5. COMMON PEOPLE VS. THE ELITE
Tolkien believed in the power of common people. This can be seen most clearly in the hobbits. They are weak and often foolish, yet capable of great acts of heroism that amaze even the very wise and the very strong.

The opposite point of view, elitism, is also apparent in Tolkien's works. His heroes seem to be a select few, chosen for the task of saving the world from evil. The ordinary people, such as the men of Lake-town and the hobbits of the Shire, are often depicted as simple and complacent. Some people see elitism as a bad thing. Others don't: People aren't all equal, they say, and it is the responsibility of the strong to help the weak. Which view do you favor? Why?

6. IMPORTANCE OF FRIENDSHIP
It is not lofty principles but love for land and friends that gives Tolkien's characters the strength

to make the right choices in the difficult decisions they face. The evil characters, who lack this capacity for friendship, hurt their own efforts by fighting among themselves. Tolkien goes further to show that friendship should not be given just within a closed circle but should be extended to all people.

7.   EVILS OF POSSESSIVENESS

In *The Hobbit* the evils of possessiveness can be easily seen. The dwarves are corrupted by their desire for treasure, and their greed almost leads to war with men and elves. But possessiveness can also be the root of the desire to dominate others that leads to the evil in *The Lord of the Rings*. Do you know what it's like to have another person feel possessive toward you? Such people can't seem to allow you your own identity—your own free will—and are unhappy if you aren't exactly what they want you to be. Now imagine if someone felt that way about the world, wanting to make everything go his way and having the power to accomplish this. He'd hate anything that had a will of its own and would want to dominate it. He might try to enslave all mankind. If he wasn't able to force nature to his will, he might even attempt to destroy it. This is exactly what Sauron tries to do in Middle-earth; he reduces countryside to wasteland, enslaves others through the lesser Rings of power, and attempts to rule all of Middle-earth.

8.   RELATIONSHIP BETWEEN MAN AND NATURE

Nature plays an important role in Tolkien's works. Through characters like Tom Bombadil and the Ents, Tolkien seems to be saying that nature is an entity separate from ourselves, something to be re- spected, not dominated. His good characters have a great respect and love for nature, while the evil ones destroy nature. Furthermore, those who live close to nature, such as the hobbits and the elves of Lórien, seem to draw great power for good from it.

9. EVILS OF TECHNOLOGY

This is related to the previous theme, for Tolkien saw technology as something that destroys nature. Middle-earth is for the most part a pretechnological world. The only technology that exists is introduced by the forces of evil and is used in destructive ways. To Tolkien, technology represents the evils of the modern world: ugliness, depersonalization, and the separation of man from nature.

STYLE

Tolkien uses a variety of styles in his works. *The Hobbit* is mostly written in relatively simple, friendly language: "With that the hobbit turned and scuttled inside his round green door, and shut it as quickly as he dared, not to seem rude." Tolkien's use of this kind of style makes sense when you realize that the book was originally published as a children's book.

The Lord of the Rings, which had been begun as a sequel to *The Hobbit*, starts out in similar style. But Tolkien soon realized that it would be a book of much wider scope than *The Hobbit*, and, accordingly, not far into the story he introduces a more serious tone. Sometimes he uses simple, conversational speech: "When Frodo came to himself he was still clutching the Ring desperately." At other times he uses a very formal style, reminiscent of the language of both ancient epics and the Bible: "And there came Gandalf on foot and with him one cloaked in grey; and they met before the doors of the Houses of Healing."

You will find many songs or poems scattered throughout Tolkien's books. You may be tempted to skip over these songs, but take a look at them anyway. They serve important purposes. They help characterize the people singing them. They also add humor or set the mood in some scenes. In addition, Tolkien's characters at times use songs in the ancient tradition of telling tales through song, as the minstrels of medieval Europe did. Keep in mind that Tolkien did not try to write polished poetry. Instead, he tried to make his songs sound like something that his characters would make up themselves.

As a scholar of language, Tolkien has a good ear for the ways different people talk. His characters and their different races have distinctive styles of speech that reveal a lot about their personalities. Look at this exchange, for example, between Bilbo and one of the dwarves in *The Hobbit:*

> "Good-bye and good luck, wherever you fare!" said Balin at last. "If ever you visit us again, when our halls are made fair once more, then the feast shall indeed be splendid!"
>
> "If ever you are passing my way," said Bilbo, "don't wait to knock! Tea is at four; but any of you are welcome at any time!"

As you can see, the main characteristic of Tolkien's style is to use language in a variety of ways. He even invented languages for his different races, such as the elves and the dwarves. You may find it interesting to choose a scene that you especially like and read it closely, noting the various ways that Tolkien uses words.

Tolkien also used other techniques of style, such as personification, metaphor, and imagery. These are discussed at various points in The Story section of this guide.

POINT OF VIEW

Tolkien's works are written in the third person and sound as though they are stories being told aloud. In *The Hobbit*, the narrator speaks as if he's telling a story to children, often interrupting himself to make little asides. He also creates a very clear moral framework for the story, telling you from the onset whether a character is good or bad or somewhere in between. This is appropriate for children, who usually want to be able to easily differentiate good and evil characters. In *The Lord of the Rings*, which is intended for adults, Tolkien no longer does this. Instead he remains for the most part outside the story, leaving it up to the characters to judge each other.

The narrator usually follows the story through the eyes of one of the hobbits. This serves two purposes. First, the hobbit is generally considered to be a representative of the modern world, a comfortably familiar character you can identify with in a book filled with such magical images as wizards and elves. Second, following the story from the hobbits' point of view makes the hobbits the heroes of the book, placing an emphasis on their traits and their way of looking at the world. In this way,

Tolkien shows the importance of ordinary people and reveals what it is that he believes makes them so special.

While the narrator of these books generally follows the story from the point of view of a character, he's not limited by that character's knowledge. He's able to step out of the story and offer information and insights that the characters are not aware of. In this way he's able to show you the total picture, which can reveal a clear pattern and purpose behind seemingly random events, while at the same time he shows how these events appear to the individuals involved.

FORM AND STRUCTURE

The Hobbit and *The Lord of the Rings* are similar in structure. Both are organized around the idea of a journey into the unknown and back again, making the stories circular in form. Each journey can be roughly divided into four parts: a period of initiation, the fulfillment of a quest, a battle or battles, and the return home.

In the first part, the inexperienced hero of the story sets out on a journey with a group of companions. The story progresses from one safe haven to another, with dangerous episodes in between. In *The Hobbit*, for example, Bilbo and the dwarves set out from Bilbo's comfortable home into the Wilds. After facing the trolls, they arrive in Rivendell, where they replenish their supplies. They are attacked by goblins while crossing the Misty Mountains, and at last reach the safety of Beorn's home. From there they pass through the dangers of Mirkwood and arrive in Lake-town. Frodo and his friends have a similar series of adventures in *The Fellowship of the Ring*, the first part of *The Lord of the Rings*.

These adventures serve as a period of initiation: through them, Bilbo and Frodo are prepared for the tasks that still await them. These entertaining episodes also give Tolkien an opportunity to present characters and themes.

The safe havens serve a similar function, introducing themes and characters. In contrast to the action of the other scenes, they provide a "tableaux," a graphic representation of a place or culture. This is especially true of *The Lord of the Rings*, with its pictures of Rivendell, Lórien, and Fangorn Forest, just to name a few. These places add to the sense of the history and cultures of Middle-earth and place the plot within the framework of this history. Many people believe that this balance between the fast-paced action of the here and now and the slow, grand sweep of history is part of what makes Tolkien's books stand out as something more than just adventure stories.

The second part of each story concerns the fulfillment of the quest, where the hero faces his moment of truth. (Bilbo's part in the quest is to help recover the treasure; Frodo's quest is to destroy the Ring.) Each must confront his fears and conquer them alone. It is at this point that the character appears as a truly heroic figure.

The third part of the story concerns a war between the forces of good and evil. (In *The Lord of the Rings*, you will notice, the story of the quest and the story of the war are intertwined.) The good side seems hopelessly outclassed, but somehow manages to emerge victorious at the last minute.

Tolkien has been building to this moment from the beginning of the story. Each preceding episode also seemed bound for disaster. Each time, the danger has become more grim, and the hope of rescue has steadily decreased, until the hero has only himself to rely on. As the danger increases, so does the level of excitement until yet another daring escape is managed.

In *The Hobbit* the danger and the excitement reach a peak when the forces of good seem about to be overcome by the forces of evil. In *The Lord of the Rings*, Tolkien builds to two simultaneous peaks. One occurs at the point when Sauron's forces sweep down on the small army led by Aragorn at the gates of Mordor. The other occurs inside Mordor, as Frodo struggles with Gollum on the edge of the Crack of Doom, where the Ring is to be destroyed. Both the war and the quest reach their resolution in the same instant, when the Ring is destroyed and with it, Sauron's power.

The fourth and final part of each story serves to wind things down. The hero returns home, looking forward to comfort. He finds instead that his home is threatened. But he has grown through his experiences and is able to regain what is his.

Of course, there are many important differences between the two works. *The Hobbit* follows the story through Bilbo's eyes and tells of events in a chronological sequence. In other words, you hear about things as they happen, rather than jumping ahead to future events, or flashing back to something that happened in the past. When Tolkien departs from this chronological sequence in *The Hobbit*, he carefully guides you through the jump in time: ''Now if you wish, like the dwarves, to hear news of

Smaug, you must go back again to the evening when he smashed the door and flew off in a rage, two days before."

The story line of *The Lord of the Rings*, on the other hand, is much more complicated. *The Lord of the Rings* is a trilogy, consisting of three volumes (Parts One to Three) divided into six sections (Books I through VI). The novel jumps back and forth in time, following the stories of several characters. The various story lines finally converge near the end when all the characters are reunited as Aragorn is crowned king of Gondor. Tolkien uses these shifts in viewpoint to good effect, often ending his scenes as cliff-hangers, slowly building the tension to its climax. But trying to follow the different story lines as he jumps back and forth from one to the other can be very difficult. Tolkien doesn't guide you through them as he did in *The Hobbit.* But he does give clues to help you put the pieces in order. For example, when Tolkien returns to Sam and Frodo in Book VI, he shows you that he's jumping back in time by telling you what Merry, Pippin, and Aragorn are doing at the same moment.

Many people have commented that *The Hobbit* is like a simple fairy tale, whereas *The Lord of the Rings* is more like a great epic poem of the past, such as *The Odyssey* of Homer or *Beowulf*, the famous Old English tale of heroism. Like both fairy tales and epics, Tolkien's books are stories of heroism in an imaginary world filled with fantastic people and creatures. But *The Hobbit*, like many fairy tales, is first and foremost the story of an individual's growth into maturity. It has a fairy-tale ending, with Bilbo smoking happily on his pipe many years later, rich from his adventures and satisfied with his life. An epic, on the other hand, tries to relate the hero's story to a long history and is more concerned with questions of moral choices and the fate of all men, than with its individual hero. In fact, many epics, such as *Beowulf,* end with the death of their heroes. *The Lord of the Rings* shares these characteristics of epics. Unlike Bilbo, Frodo doesn't live happily ever after. He's been wounded physically and also psychically by the loss of the Ring. His passage to the Blessed Realm at the end of the book may be interpreted as a symbolic death.

Part of Tolkien's genius lies in the way he combined the forms of fairy tale and epic. The heroes of most epics are larger than life, possessing great strength and ability, like the superheroes of comic books. But people nowadays find it hard to identify with such impossible heroes. Frodo, an ordinary person who has been thrust into a situation beyond his abilities, is a more suitable hero for a modern audience. Aragorn, on the other hand, is a classic epic hero. But he has a fairy-tale ending, winning a kingdom and marrying his lifelong love. So you see, Tolkien didn't just copy the old forms of fairy tale and epic. He reworked them to meet the needs of a modern audience. From the great success of his books, he seems to have achieved his goal.

THE STORIES

In this discussion, the chapters in *The Hobbit* and *The Lord of the Rings* are grouped into sections. The sections in *The Hobbit* correspond to the series of adventures of Bilbo. Tolkien himself divided *The Lord of the Rings* into six sections, or books. In our discussion of the story, each of the six books is further divided into two roughly equal parts.

The Hobbit
CHAPTERS 1–3

Bilbo sets out on his adventure with Gandalf and the dwarves. After a near-fatal encounter with three trolls, the travelers arrive in the haven of Rivendell.

*

Bilbo Baggins is a well-to-do, respectable hobbit who lives alone in his tidy hobbit-hole. The comfortable order of his life is disrupted one day when Gandalf the wizard and thirteen dwarves arrive at his door. Trying to act as though nothing is out of the ordinary, Bilbo invites them in for tea and cakes. Bilbo's predicament is amusing to many readers, as he runs around red-faced and flustered, answering the doorbell and serving his uninvited guests.

This kind of humor is one aspect of Tolkien's style that some readers dislike, finding it too childish and simple. Others consider it delightful. It serves an important purpose, however. You may find the existence of dwarves, wizards, and hobbits hard to accept. Tolkien anticipates that reaction and gently ridicules his characters, hoping to disarm you. He doesn't yet require you to take them seriously.

NOTE: The Origins of Hobbits   The best information on how Tolkien developed his hobbits comes from the author himself: "The Hobbits are just rustic English people, made small in size because it reflects the generally small reach of their imagination—not the small reach of their courage or latent power." He also admitted to what may seem a surprising literary source, the novel *Babbitt* by Sinclair Lewis, an unsympathetic portrayal of an American businessman. How does the main character in that book relate to Tolkien's hobbits? According to Tolkien, "Babbitt has the same bourgeois smugness that hobbits do. His world is the same limited place."

Unlike Sinclair Lewis and Babbitt, Tolkien portrays his hobbits in a sympathetic light. Tolkien often compared himself to hobbits and once said, "[They were] just what I could have liked to have been, but never was." You may wonder why anyone would want to be like Bilbo Baggins. You will have to wait to see what it is that makes hobbits so special to Tolkien and hobbit fans.

Thorin, the dwarves' self-important leader, is the grandson of Thrain, who once ruled a kingdom of dwarves under the Lonely Mountain. One day a dragon named Smaug descended on the mountain, killing most of the dwarves and stealing their treasure. Now Thorin and the other twelve dwarves intend to return to the mountain, avenge their kin, and recover the treasure.

Gandalf has picked Bilbo to be their burglar, but the dwarves aren't too happy with the wizard's choice. Bilbo certainly doesn't seem very qualified for the job. He's a timid little fellow who faints at the talk of danger. But Gandalf says that there's more to Bilbo than even Bilbo realizes. Under Gandalf's fierce gaze, the dwarves relent. But have they really accepted the hobbit?

Bilbo doesn't seem to be too sure that he wants to be a burglar. Part of him longs for adventure, but another part wants to be left alone to enjoy his comfortable life. What do you think makes him decide to join the dwarves?

In the morning, Bilbo and the dwarves get on their way. After a pleasant start, they face the first of many dangers on their journey. As a cold, rainy evening sets in, they discover that Gandalf has left them. Then they see a light among the trees ahead, and Bilbo is sent to investigate, supposedly because he's the burglar. With a hobbit's knack for walking silently, he approaches the fire without being seen. There he finds three huge trolls. Instead of going back to report to the dwarves, he attempts to pick the pocket of one of the trolls and is captured. Soon the dwarves are captured as well.

The scene with the trolls has some good examples of how Tolkien lets his characters describe themselves through their actions and their speech, a commendable element of good fiction writing. Bilbo walks "primly" through the trees and sniffs at the dwarves' noisiness. What kind of person does that bring to mind? And you get a good idea of what the trolls are like by the way they eat and speak.

What do you think of the dwarves so far? They seem to be taking advantage of Bilbo when they send him ahead, but they're also quick to come help him. Thorin is almost heroic when he valiantly takes on all three trolls to save his friends. But he too ends up tied in a sack like the others. The dwarves apparently have bungled the rescue as badly as Bilbo bungled his pickpocket attempt.

Fortunately, Gandalf returns and rescues his friends through a clever bit of ventriloquism. By imitating the voice of first one troll and then another, he manages to keep them arguing until dawn, when they are turned to stone. Before going on, Gandalf and Thorin take swords from the trolls' hoard. Bilbo picks up a dagger that suits him well as a sword.

Gandalf leads the band to Rivendell, where Elrond, chief of the Half-elven, lives. In the ancient tales that Tolkien studied, elves were a race of beautiful and magical people. But since then, elves have come to be thought of as tiny, mischievous creatures who live in flower buds and ride in coaches drawn by insects. Tolkien tried to restore elves to their original stature.

When Bilbo and the dwarves arrive in Rivendell, the elves at first appear foolish, singing silly songs and laughing merrily. But Tolkien warns you that it is unwise to let yourself be deceived by appearances. Through the wise and noble character of Elrond, he reveals the more heroic aspect of elves. You learn that long ago they fought beside men in a great war against the goblins. The swords that Gandalf and Thorin took from the trolls' hoard had been made by the High Elves to be used in that war.

NOTE: The Naming of Swords   In ancient tales, most heroes named their swords. King Arthur's sword, for example, was called Excalibur. By giving names to Thorin and Gandalf's swords, Tolkien places those warriors in the company of such great heroes. Notice that Bilbo's sword isn't mentioned, and it remains nameless. Do you think there is any significance in this?

CHAPTERS 4–6

The travelers are captured by goblins in the Misty Mountains. In the goblin tunnels, Bilbo finds a magic ring and meets its previous owner, Gollum. With the help of the ring, Bilbo escapes the tunnels and rejoins his friends.

*

Days later, Thorin and the company cross the Misty Mountains and are attacked by goblins. All but Gandalf are captured and carried through a maze of tunnels into the heart of the mountain. Tolkien tells you that the goblins are "cruel, wicked, and bad-hearted," and in his description of them you can see the beginnings of his concept of evil. Their hatred of others is an important part of evil. They deny others free will by enslaving them, and they create nothing of beauty. Tolkien also makes an association here between evil and technology, particularly the technology of war—"the ingenious devices for killing large numbers of people at once."

NOTE: Tolkien's Use of Song   One of the purposes of songs in *The Hobbit* is to characterize the different races. In chapter 1, the dwarves' song expresses their love for treasure. The elves' song in chapter 3 expresses their gaiety. The song that

the goblins sing is reminiscent of pirates and reveals their cruelty. The many one-syllable words
and exclamation points give it a savage rhythm
that Tolkien echoes in the narrative and in the
speech of the Great Goblin.

Once again, Gandalf comes to the rescue. He
kills the Great Goblin and leads Bilbo and the
dwarves down the tunnels. Notice how Tolkien
uses personification to describe Gandalf's sword.
It "burned with a rage" at the presence of goblins
and now gleams "bright as blue flame for delight"
in killing their leader.

The angry goblins chase after their escaping
prisoners. In the confusion, Bilbo falls, bumps his
head, and is knocked unconscious.

When he wakes up, Bilbo finds himself alone in
the dark. While groping around blindly, he comes
upon a ring and slips it into his pocket. Tolkien
tells you that this is a turning point in Bilbo's ca-
reer, but doesn't say why.

Bilbo searches in his pockets for matches to light
his pipe. He doesn't find them but does come upon
his sword, which he draws out. This action is highly
significant, for while smoking a pipe just then would
have been both stupid and hobbitlike, the decision
to draw his sword could be a sign of Bilbo's growing independence. He sets off down the tunnel
and at an underground lake meets Gollum, one of
Tolkien's most unforgettable creations.

It is Gollum's speech that is most remarkable.
He hisses as he talks, and calls himself "we" and
"my precious." He never speaks directly to Bilbo;
he talks to himself and refers to Bilbo as "it." This

way of speaking shows the selfishness of evil: Gollum treats Bilbo as an object—a potential meal—rather than as an individual with free will. In accordance with Tolkien's theme that nothing starts out evil, Gollum was once a sun-loving creature like Bilbo. For some reason not yet disclosed to the reader, Gollum was driven from his home and eventually found his way to the lake in the middle of the mountain. (You will learn more about Gollum's life, such as how he came to the underground lake, in *The Lord of the Rings*.)

NOTE: Riddle games   Back in the times when people first told the legends of King Arthur and Siegfried the dragon-killer, they didn't have as much in the way of entertainment as we do today. Instead, they had to entertain themselves. One way they did this was by playing riddle games. The first person who failed to answer a riddle lost the game. Riddle games were so popular that they became a common feature in folklore and legend. In these legendary games the stakes were often high: the loser would forfeit a valuable magical treasure or even his life. Tolkien drew directly on these stories when he devised the riddle game between Gollum and Bilbo. In this case, if Bilbo loses, Gollum will eat him. Fortunately, Bilbo manages to stump Gollum with an unorthodox riddle: "What have I got in my pocket?" (This leads some people to question whether Bilbo won the game fairly.) The other riddles that appear in this scene are old standards, not only in Middle-earth but also in our own world. In fact, many of these riddles were favorites of the ancient Norse and Anglo-Saxons, and can be found in their writings that have been preserved through the centuries.

The ring that Bilbo discovered belongs to Gollum, who lost it hunting goblins in the tunnel. Gollum is obsessed with his ring, calling it by the name he uses for himself: "my precious." He lets out a horrible screech when he realizes it's gone and Bilbo has it. He rushes toward Bilbo in a murderous rage. Bilbo flees, and the ring somehow slips onto his finger.

As he runs down the dark tunnel, Bilbo trips and falls, but Gollum continues past him. Realizing the ring has made him invisible, Bilbo uses it to escape Gollum and slip out the goblins' back door. Gollum shrieks after Bilbo: "Thief, thief, thief! Baggins! We hates it, we hates it, we hates it for ever!" Is Bilbo a thief? Do you feel any sympathy for Gollum? Why or why not?

NOTE: Responsible Use of Power   The ring represents great power. Gollum used it to sneak up on goblins and kill them, and had planned to use it in the same way to kill Bilbo. Bilbo could also have used the ring against Gollum, but instead he jumps over Gollum's head and runs away. He does this both out of sympathy for Gollum and because of his sense of fair play. Do you think he's foolish to take such a chance?

Bilbo emerges from the goblin tunnels and realizes that he's come through all the way to the other side of the mountain. Alone, with no idea what has happened to his friends, he decides to go back into the tunnels to find them. Just then he hears the voices of his companions. Since he's wearing the ring, the others can't see him. As he approaches, the dwarves are saying that they don't want to go back to find Bilbo, while Gandalf is insisting that they must. Bilbo takes off his ring and suddenly appears, surprising them all.

Here Tolkien shows you Bilbo as morally superior to the dwarves. He was willing to go back into the tunnels alone to try to find them, but they prefer to leave him to the goblins rather than to risk getting caught themselves. You may say that the dwarves are just being realistic and that Bilbo is naively idealistic. How does this relate to Tolkien's theme that you must do what is right, no matter what the consequences?

Bilbo tells about his encounter with Gollum but doesn't mention the ring. The dwarves are greatly impressed. Gandalf gives Bilbo a queer look, as if he suspects Bilbo hasn't told the whole truth.

Knowing the goblins will pursue once night falls, the adventurers travel well into the night. They stop at last, but soon hear the howling of wolves. As they scramble into trees, a pack of wolves run into the clearing.

These are no ordinary wolves. They are Wargs, allies of the goblins, and Bilbo and his friends are trapped.

Far away, the Lord of the Eagles hears the commotion and with his followers decides to investigate.

Meanwhile, the goblins arrive in the clearing. Gandalf prepares to jump down among them and kill as many as he can before he dies. Just then, the eagles arrive and carry Bilbo and the others off to their home on the mountain peak. There the eagles bring them food: animals, which the dwarves prepare and cook. Tolkien again emphasizes how out of place Bilbo is with the dwarves. He doesn't know how to skin and cut up meat; he's used to having it delivered by the butcher!

CHAPTERS 7–9

After enjoying the hospitality of Beorn, the shape-changer, Bilbo and the dwarves travel through Mirkwood Forest. Bilbo has an opportunity to prove himself by twice coming to the dwarves' rescue.

*

The next morning, the eagles deliver the travelers to the top of a great rock near the house of someone named Beorn. Gandalf warns the company that Beorn, a very great man, is easily angered; they must be very polite to him.

Beorn, whom Gandalf describes as part bear, part man, gives the group food and advice for their journey: They will have to travel through the terrible forest of Mirkwood, but should stay on the path and *not* drink or bathe in the water of a certain stream. He also gives them ponies but asks that they be returned when the travelers reach the edge of the woods.

NOTE: Beorn is a typical hero of the old legends. He is self-assured and seldom polite. He's also extremely fierce, almost bloodthirsty, as shown by the goblin head on the post outside his house. Unlike the ancient heroes, however, Beorn seems to belong more to the world of animals than to the world of men. He speaks with his animals, who are friends rather than possessions. He associates with bears and can turn into one himself. On the other hand, he tries to avoid people, never liking more than one visitor at a time. In *The Lord of the Rings* you'll find other characters who, like Beorn, are closely associated with nature.

The company reaches Mirkwood in four days. The dwarves want to keep the ponies, but Gandalf insists they be sent back. Then Gandalf says good-bye, and Bilbo and the dwarves are on their own.

As the band travels through the eerie forest of Mirkwood, Bilbo has an opportunity to convincingly prove his worth to the others. At one point, he becomes separated from the band. A giant spider attacks him and—alone and in the dark—he kills it with his sword. This serves as an initiation for Bilbo, and, proud of his victory, he finally names his sword; he calls it Sting.

Feeling bolder, Bilbo searches for his friends, only to find them prisoners of the spiders. Using his ring to become invisible, he sings insulting songs about the spiders and frees enough of the band so they can fight their way to safety. This is the first time Bilbo has made up a song, and it's the beginning of his transition into the heroic world, where the use of songs and the naming of swords are commonplace.

Bilbo has won the respect of the dwarves. Even

though he has had to reveal the secret of the ring, they admire his courage and ingenuity in using it. They begin to look to him for help, just as they used to look to Gandalf. Then suddenly they realize Thorin is missing. It's too dark to look for him, so they go to sleep with this new trouble on their minds.

We learn that Thorin has been captured by Wood-elves, who, though good, are not friendly to dwarves. Knowing their king is greedy for treasure, Thorin refuses to answer his questions and is imprisoned.

As they wander in the forest the next evening, the rest of the dwarves are captured by the Wood-elves. Bilbo evades capture by slipping on his ring. The captives are taken to the king's palace and imprisoned when they refuse to answer questions. Bilbo, invisible, wanders around the palace. Ironically, he now lives up to his role as burglar, sneaking around and stealing food. He finds the imprisoned dwarves, who are quite confident the hobbit will rescue them. Bilbo isn't so hopeful and wishes that Gandalf were around. But with growing maturity, he realizes that if the dwarves are to be rescued, he must do it himself. You can see that Bilbo has grown from a helpless, foolish hobbit into someone who can take responsibility not only for himself, but for the lives of others. And yet Bilbo is also dependent on the dwarves; he wouldn't know where to go or what to do without them.

With a great deal of luck and ingenuity, Bilbo manages to free his friends, then packs them into empty barrels, which the elves throw into a stream that runs under the palace. They all float off down the stream, with Bilbo clinging to an empty barrel.

NOTE: Much is made of Bilbo's luck in this chapter. Yet it was not merely luck that made him successful: Bilbo was prepared to take advantage of his luck. Throughout *The Hobbit* and *The Lord of the Rings,* watch for other instances where luck serves to help individuals who are already trying to help themselves.

CHAPTERS 10–13

Bilbo and the dwarves are helped by the people of Lake-town, which lies in the shadow of the Lonely Mountain. The adventurers at last reach the mountain, and Bilbo comes face to face with the dragon Smaug.

*

The barrels, along with Bilbo and the dwarves, have floated down the river to Lake-town, in the shadow of the Lonely Mountain where Smaug the dragon lives. The arrival of the dwarves, after Bilbo frees them from the barrels, sparks great excitement. The town had been very prosperous before the coming of Smaug, and old songs predict that good times would return with the dwarves. People begin to sing the old songs and say that the prophecy will be fulfilled. Treated like heroes, the dwarves are given a large house and good food, and are wildly cheered in public.

The warm reception the dwarves receive may seem odd to you. After all, they haven't done anything yet. But traditionally there is a certain type of hero who is rewarded before the deed. This is the person who is about to undertake a great task for the sake of his people, and who is as likely to die in the attempt as to return successfully. The first U.S. astronauts in the late 1950s were such heroes, receiving great fame and adulation before the first mission was ever launched.

The dwarves at last depart for the Lonely Mountain with ponies and supplies provided by the town. They are given a warm send-off and everyone is in high spirits—everyone, that is, except Bilbo, who's very unhappy at the thought of approaching Smaug's lair. This is reminiscent of Gandalf, who is wise enough to be aware of dangers even when everyone else forgets them.

The land around the Lonely Mountain has been desolated by the dragon. The dwarves are grim and sad as they remember how beautiful it once was. Yet, as their spirits droop, Bilbo's seem to lift. He studies Thorin's map and convinces the dwarves to search for the secret door. At last they find it, far up the mountain's slope, but they lose hope again when they fail to open the door. They blame Bilbo (since he's the burglar) and consider sending him through the front gate of the dragon's lair.

Once again it's Bilbo who takes charge and solves their problems. He remembers the secret runes (mysterious writing) that Elrond had discovered on the map. Just as the runes said, the last ray of the sun reveals the keyhole to the secret door, and at last the way is open.

You see how much the dwarves have come to rely on Bilbo. He has in effect become their leader. Yet does he get the respect due a leader? Why do you think the dwarves treat him the way they do?

In chapter 12, Bilbo twice ventures down the secret passage to the lair of Smaug. The first time, the dwarves send him, saying that it's time for him to be the burglar. This is similar to the scene in chapter 2, where they send him to investigate the trolls' fire. But there are several important differences between the two episodes that clearly show the changes in Bilbo. He is now more assertive with the dwarves, pointing out that he's already won his share of the treasure by rescuing them twice. But he says he'll go anyway—he's begun to trust his luck more—and dares any of the dwarves to come with him. Do you agree with the narrator's defense of the dwarves' refusal to go with him (except for Balin, who goes part of the way)—that it's Bilbo's job for which he'll be paid very well?

Bilbo is terrified but determined to see things through. When he hears the rumbling of the dragon's breath, he pauses for a moment. Facing his fear and going on despite it is the bravest thing he's ever done. This sort of courage is the basis of Tolkien's idea of heroism, which he sees as something internal, rather than as the doing of great deeds. Once Bilbo reaches Smaug's lair, he successfully steals a cup from the dragon's hoard and carries it back with him. (Compare this to his bungling in the scene with the trolls.)

Smaug awakes to discover the cup is missing. He goes on a rampage, searching the mountainside for the thief. Some of the dwarves risk their lives to rescue two of their company who had stayed with the ponies further down the mountain. What do you think Tolkien is trying to tell you through this act of heroism by the dwarves? Is there a limit to the dwarves' kind of heroism?

Bilbo goes down to the dragon's lair once again—

but this time on his own initiative. He has a conversation with the wily Smaug and holds his own admirably. Smaug is the essence of politeness, yet full of veiled threat. Bilbo intrigues him with riddles by giving himself many names that refer to his adventures. Barrel-rider, for example, refers to his escape from the Wood-elves. (This kind of name-giving is a common habit among heroes of legend and folklore.) Smaug tries to plant suspicions in Bilbo's mind against the dwarves, but the hobbit remains true to his friends. Is all that Smaug says untrue? Bilbo cleverly tricks Smaug into revealing a bare spot in his armor of gems. With a parting taunt Bilbo leaves, getting his hair and heels singed for his boldness.

NOTE: Dragons in Legend and Literature   Smaug has been compared most often to Fafnir, a dragon from the Scandinavian legends, and to the dragon in *Beowulf*. Both these famous dragons brood over a treasure, Fafnir in a cave, and the other in a castle. The hero Sigurd comes seeking Fafnir's treasure, and the dragon engages him first in conversation. A wily talker like Smaug, Fafnir manages to raise suspicions in Sigurd's mind about the trustworthiness of his companions. Fafnir is killed when Sigurd hides in a hole and thrusts his sword into the dragon's soft belly. The fire-breathing dragon in *Beowulf* ravages the countryside in a rage after a thief steals a single cup from his great hoard. Beowulf, as leader of his people, undertakes the task of killing this menace. He succeeds but is mortally wounded by the dragon.

Tolkien drew on both these stories in *The Hobbit*.

He also drew on the common association of dragons with the destruction of landscapes (the desolation by Smaug), with the possession of one vulnerable spot, with the insatiable desire for material possessions, and with evil (some dragons were thought to be the Devil himself).

Bilbo tells his tale to the dwarves, while a thrush listens nearby. Remember this bird, because it will become an important part of the plot in chapter 14. Bilbo grows increasingly uneasy about the dragon, and at his insistence the company hides in the secret passage. They shut the door—just in time, for Smaug attacks the doorway. They're trapped, but at least they're still alive. Meanwhile Smaug, satisfied he's taken care of the intruders, departs for Lake-town.

After what seems days of waiting, with no hint of Smaug's presence, the dwarves follow Bilbo down the tunnel to the dragon's lair. Bilbo ventures into the dark cavern alone and in the light of a torch discovers the Arkenstone. Thorin had spoken of this great jewel the night before. It had been mined from the Lonely Mountain and is greatly prized by the dwarves. Bilbo hides it in his pocket, not telling the dwarves of his discovery.

The dwarves are excited by the sight of so much treasure. They clad themselves in armor from the hoard and give a suit of mail to Bilbo. Bilbo feels magnificent wearing it, but suspects he looks silly. Unlike the dwarves, he's not bewitched by the treasure, realizing that they're not yet out of trouble. You can see how Bilbo remains down-to-earth, not carried away by the situations he finds himself in. Neither does he get caught up in visions of himself as a great hero in his armor. Thoughts of home help him keep things in perspective.

CHAPTERS 14–17

After Smaug is killed by a man of Lake-town, an army of men and elves sets out for the mountain to recover Smaug's hoard. Instead they find the dwarves in possession of the treasure. The dispute over the wealth is about to erupt into war when an army of goblins and Wargs attacks.

*

Tolkien takes you back to the night that Smaug destroyed the secret door, trapping the dwarves inside the passage. After doing so, Smaug descends on Lake-town, which Tolkien now calls by the name Esgaroth. (This sudden switch in name is unexplained.) The townspeople resist at first, but faced by Smaug's wrath, they soon flee. The Master of the town sneaks off in his boat, trying to save himself. Only a small band of archers hold their ground, led by a man named Bard. Bard is descended from the lord of Dale, who was killed when Smaug first drove the dwarves from the Lonely Mountain and destroyed the town of Dale. Bard refuses to quit what seems a hopeless battle, even though his companions are ready to leave him. Suddenly a thrush—the same bird who listened to Bilbo tell the dwarves about his conversation with the dragon—perches on Bard's shoulder and reveals the vulnerable spot that Bilbo had discovered in Smaug's armor. Bard fits his last arrow to his bow and kills the dragon. Smaug plunges into the lake, destroying the town.

The townspeople now turn on the Master for

abandoning the town. They talk of making Bard their king. But the Master cleverly diverts them by turning their anger toward the dwarves, saying that they aroused Smaug in the first place. He also declares that if Bard is to be king he should rebuild the ruins of Dale and rule there, not in Lake-town. For now, Bard takes the lead in making sure the people of Lake-town have shelter and food. He sends a messenger to the king of the Wood-elves asking for help.

NOTE: The Ideal Leader In comparing Bard to the Master of Lake-town, Tolkien presents his ideas about an ideal leader. Bard becomes a leader by proving himself as a warrior; the Master leads by virtue of his business acumen. Bard, a true leader, is willing to risk his life to save the town; the Master places his own interests and safety above those of his people. Tolkien is making a point that a leader should serve his people rather than use his position to further his own ends. Bard speaks openly, even saying things that others don't want to hear, as when he warns them that death, rather than wealth, may result from the dwarves' expedition to the mountain. The Master, on the other hand, tells his people what they want to hear and manipulates them by appealing to baser emotions such as greed and desire for revenge. What are the characteristics of other leaders that appear in *The Hobbit*? In what ways are they like Bard or like the Master? Keep the image of a grim warrior-leader in mind, for it will reappear in *The Lord of the Rings* in the character of Aragorn.

The Elvenking has already received news of

Smaug's death from the birds and is journeying with a large host toward the Lonely Mountain to seize the dragon's hoard of treasure. But he turns aside to help the lake people. What does this tell you about the Wood-elves? Do you find your attitude toward them changing? The building of a new town is begun under the Master's direction. The elves, accompanied by Bard and his men, set out for the Lonely Mountain.

The dwarves are not caught unaware, for they are told of Smaug's death and the approaching army by ravens, who have long been friends with the race of dwarves. Although the ancient chief of the ravens advises them to make peace, the dwarves begin to fortify the approach to the mountain. Messages are sent to Thorin's relatives asking for help.

When the Lake-men and the elves finally arrive, Bard claims the share of the treasure that was stolen from the town of Dale. Thorin refuses, and so the army of men and elves besieges the mountain.

In chapter 15, Tolkien hints at the tragedy of war. The dwarves hear music from the camp and wish they could have welcomed these enemies as friends. Bilbo longs to be among the elves, feasting and laughing. Why then do the dwarves refuse to parley? Is it only their greed for treasure, as the narrator seems to imply, or do you think that some of Thorin's arguments are valid?

Not at all happy with the prospect of war, Bilbo comes up with a plan to try to prevent it. Putting on his ring and carrying the Arkenstone, he slips away from the dwarves. He brings the stone to Bard, hoping it can be used to bargain with Thorin.

Bard, the Elvenking, and Gandalf, who reappears in the elves' camp, praise the hobbit for his action. Then Bilbo returns to the dwarves' camp.

It may seem strange to you that Bilbo should return to the dwarves, who will certainly be angry with what he's done. But Bilbo will not desert his friends. To understand this is to understand much of Tolkien's idea of the greatness of the common people. Bilbo has very simple values and stands by them. One thing he values highly is friends. Another thing he values highly is the comfortable life he led in Bag End. Throughout the adventure Bilbo keeps thinking of his home, enabling him to keep things in perspective, something the dwarves have failed to do. He realizes that the dwarves' gold isn't much good without food or without the friendship of their neighbors. He just wants to see the whole thing come to an end, and this is what prompts him to give up the Arkenstone.

Bard reveals to Thorin that he has the Arkenstone. In his anger Thorin almost throws Bilbo over the wall. Thorin reluctantly agrees to give up one-fourteenth of the treasure—Bilbo's share—in return for the Arkenstone. While Bilbo goes down to join Gandalf, Thorin is already thinking of a way to go back on his word. Dain, his cousin, is now approaching with an army of dwarves. Thorin wonders if he can recapture the Arkenstone with Dain's help and avoid paying Bilbo's share of the treasure. In chapter 14, Tolkien had said that the dwarves were affected by the bewitchment of the treasure. Now he says something similar when he attributes Thorin's actions to the *bewilderment* of the treasure. What do you think Tolkien is implying?

When Dain arrives, he finds his way barred by the other army, and he attacks. But a new army suddenly appears, made up of goblins and Wargs. Their quarrels forgotten, Dain's army joins with the men and elves to meet this new foe. Despite valiant resistance on the part of the combined forces, the goblins seem assured of victory. Bilbo contemplates the idea of defeat. In old songs and legends it is said that defeat is glorious, but Bilbo finds it very distressing. Tolkien at this point speaks from his own experience in the Battle of the Somme.

The attack of the goblins is in some ways beneficial, for it prevents a tragic war between races who should be allies. Squabbles over gold are shown to be petty. The forces of good unite against a common evil, in a desperate fight for survival. In this fight, even Thorin and his companions are able to redeem themselves.

As a sign of the change in the dwarves, from petty greed to noble courage, Tolkien uses heroic language to describe them. "Hood and cloak were gone; they were in shining armour, and red light leapt from their eyes. In the gloom the great dwarf gleamed like gold in a dying fire." The second sentence even has the rhythms of the Old English poetry that Tolkien admired. Notice too, the many words beginning with "g" in that sentence. This is an example of alliteration. Old English poetry, which doesn't use rhymes at the end of lines, relies on such techniques as alliteration and meter (or rhythm) to give the poem its characteristic sound. Sentences such as this reveal Tolkien's painstaking craftsmanship, which may go unnoticed on first reading.

NOTE: Dwarves in Lore and Literature   In the beginning of *The Hobbit*, Tolkien's dwarves seem to have come right out of the fairy tale *Snow White and the Seven Dwarfs*. But like elves, the dwarves of fairy tales have degenerated greatly from their origins in myth and legends. In *The Hobbit*, Tolkien reverses that course, elevating his dwarves from comic characters to heroic figures.

The names of Tolkien's dwarves, as well as the wizard's name (Gandalf), come from a list of dwarves in an ancient book of Norse mythology, *The Prose Edda*, by Snorri Sturlson. This book was an attempt to preserve the pagan beliefs and lore that were rapidly disappearing in the face of Christianity's growing power in Europe. The dwarves of *The Prose Edda*, typical of traditional dwarves, were miners and expert craftsmen who lived in caves and mountains. There are many stories of dwarves who created marvelous and magical things, and in these stories the dwarves are often cheated of their pay. This may have been the inspiration for the dispute over treasure and pay between dwarves and elves in *The Hobbit*. Dwarves have also been traditionally associated with the fierce love of treasure that characterizes Tolkien's dwarves.

CHAPTERS 18–19

The war is over, and Bilbo finds that he's a hero. After many fond farewells, he heads home.

*

Bilbo, who has been knocked unconscious, comes to and finds himself alone. The war is over. He returns to camp to find Thorin dying. Wanting to make amends with Bilbo, the dwarf says, "If more of us valued food and cheer and song above hoarded gold, it would be a merrier world."

NOTE: Redemption Through Courage A recurrent theme of epics is redemption through courage. In the French epic poem *Le Chanson de Roland* ("The Song of Roland"), the hero is Roland, whose desire for prestige leads him to take unnecessary risks with his men in battle, rather than call for help. Roland's pride (a common flaw of epic heroes) leads to disaster for himself and his men. Roland redeems himself through heroism in battle, where he continues fighting even when there is no hope for victory, and dies of his wounds. Likewise, Thorin, who is guilty of greed, has redeemed himself by entering the seemingly hopeless battle, risking his life and exhibiting great courage.

Bilbo sets out for home with two chests of gold and silver, and the friendship of dwarves and elves. When Bilbo and the dwarves say good-bye, you can see how they have come to reconcile their differences. Even though Balin's farewell is stiff and formal and Bilbo's is comically casual and more modern, the message is the same: stop by and visit. Through this, Tolkien points out that, despite surface differences, there are un-

derlying similarities uniting them. Against a
common enemy, all disagreements over wealth
and all past grudges about perceived wrongs
seem petty in comparison. Friendship emerges as
something of great value.

The war has had its positive aspects. Tolkien
tells you that, in the years following, the few sur-
viving goblins hide in fear and the Wargs vanish
completely. The forces of good are free to settle
the land unmolested.

Bilbo begins his journey home, accompanied by
Gandalf, and stops in Rivendell on the way. The
songs of the elves repeat Tolkien's antiwar theme:
moonlight and starlight and a fire in the hearth are
more important than gold and silver. But they also
add a new twist: the elves, who are strongly allied
with nature, sing about nature's permanence.
Kingdoms rise and fall, yet in the valley of Rivendell the grass is still growing and the elves are
still singing.

Gandalf and Elrond reveal their awareness that
this war has not vanquished evil; evil has been
destroyed before, only to appear again in another
place. This theme may seem to be an intentional
foreshadowing of the events later told in *The Lord
of the Rings*, but it is not. Tolkien at this point had
no intention of taking the story of Bilbo and Middle-earth any further.

Still in possession of the magic ring, Bilbo returns home to find that he is presumed dead and
that his effects are being auctioned off. His adventures have prepared him to cope with this prob-
lem, however, and he soon regains possession of
Bag End.

The Lord
of the Rings

PART ONE: THE FELLOWSHIP
OF THE RING

BOOK I, CHAPTERS 1–6

Frodo Baggins inherits Bilbo's magic ring. Frodo learns that the ring belongs to the evil power, Sauron, and flees the Shire with it. He and his friends become lost in the mysterious Old Forest, where they meet Tom Bombadil.

*

Sixty years have passed since Bilbo returned from the adventure told in *The Hobbit*. He is now preparing for an extended journey, intending never to return to the Shire. He plans to give his house and the magic ring to his young cousin and heir, Frodo Baggins. Bilbo finds it difficult, however, to part with the ring.

In *The Hobbit*, Bilbo's ring seemed quite innocent, almost a toy. But already it's beginning to take on a sinister aspect. When Gandalf presses Bilbo to leave the ring behind, the hobbit becomes uncharacteristically suspicious and angry. He even calls the ring by Gollum's name for it: "My precious." There seem to be two sides to his personality—his old self who honestly means to leave the ring behind, and another self who contrives to keep it. This other self could be interpreted as Bilbo's subconscious, acting out his secret wish to keep the ring. But there's another possibility—that the ring has somehow gained a hold in his mind and is controlling his actions. Gandalf, at any rate, finds the change in Bilbo alarming, and at last convinces him to leave the ring behind. Do you think Gandalf was right to be concerned? Did he force Bilbo to leave the ring, or did Bilbo leave it of his own free will?

The story then jumps ahead almost twenty years. Gandalf visits Frodo with disturbing news. At the end of *The Hobbit*, Gandalf had mentioned that the Necromancer had been driven out of Mirkwood. Gandalf now tells Frodo that this Necromancer is none other than Sauron, an evil power believed to have been killed long ago. He has returned to his ancient stronghold in Mordor and is gathering strength to conquer Middle-earth.

NOTE: Throughout the trilogy, Tolkien uses *shadow* as a metaphor for the evil power of Sauron, giving an impression of evil as being somehow insubstantial. Yet its presence is very real. Be alert for references to *shadow* as you read, and in each case try to determine how it may relate to evil.

Sauron once had a ring of power that was taken from him at the end of the last war and subsequently lost. It was found again by a small hobbitlike creature named Déagol. He was murdered by his friend Sméagol, who used the Ring to steal and to spy on his people. Given the name Gollum, because of the gurgling sounds he made in his throat, Sméagol became so wicked that he was exiled from his home. Eventually he found his way to the Misty Mountains and made his home in a subterranean lake deep in the mountain's heart. It was there that Bilbo met Gollum and gained ownership of the Ring.

NOTE: The Ring: A Double-edged Weapon From this point, Tolkien refers to Frodo's ring as "the Ring" because of its great importance. The Ring emerges through the course of the story as a symbol of the power to control others. The Ring is a dangerous weapon, however; while it gives its wearer the power to dominate others, it also has the power to dominate those who possess it. Remember Bilbo's unwillingness to give it up?

Some readers see the Ring as a symbol for the atomic bomb. Like the Ring, the bomb is a weapon of great power, but it's also dangerous to the country that possesses it. Tolkien, however, denied that anything in his book stands for any one thing in the real world.

Gandalf says that Gollum's story is a sad one that might have happened to others, including some hobbits he has known. Do you think he's referring to Bilbo? Gandalf also comments that even Gollum wasn't wholly corrupted by the Ring: "There was a little corner of his mind that was still his own . . ." He seems to be implying that Gollum wasn't evil at first. Gandalf pities Gollum and wonders aloud if he could be cured, speaking of evil as if it's a disease. In Gandalf's story about Gollum, Tolkien introduces themes that will be repeated throughout the book: Nothing starts out evil. Those who do fall into evil are hurt by it, but it's always possible for them to be redeemed.

Sauron has learned from Gollum that his Ring was found, and for the first time he hears of hobbits and the Shire. Sauron will come looking for the Ring, Gandalf tells Frodo. When he made the Ring, Sauron put most of his power into it, and without it his strength is limited. If he can recover the Ring, no one will be able to stop him. To keep Sauron from getting it, the Ring must be destroyed.

NOTE: The Ring must be destroyed because of its power to corrupt even the best of individuals. In this way it is similar to a treasure appearing in another novel, John Steinbeck's *The Pearl*. In that book a pearl of great value is found by a poor Mexican Indian. He finds that it's a curse rather than a blessing, however. The pearl appeals to the greed in others, who resort to apalling acts of violence in an attempt to possess it. In the end the Indian casts the pearl back into the sea, where it can no longer incite men to evil. The pearl symbolizes the corrupting lure of wealth, while the Ring symbolizes the corrupting effect of power.

Frodo tries to give the Ring to Gandalf, who refuses to take it. The Ring would corrupt even him; he would not be able to resist the temptation to use it for good. And Gandalf is sure that once he used it, the Ring would gain power over him and he'd become another Dark Lord, like Sauron.

Also, Gandalf says, Frodo was meant to have

the Ring. He has been chosen by some higher will that has power for good in the world. But Gandalf emphasizes that it's Frodo's choice to accept or reject this destiny. Tolkien introduces two more of his themes here. One is that there is a benevolent force at work that opposes the power of evil, and that everyone has a role to play in its grand design. The other is that individuals should not be forced to do anything—even to follow their roles in the grand scheme of things. For good or bad, all people must be free to make their own choices.

Frodo is woefully unprepared for the challenge. At first he thinks the Ring can be destroyed with a hammer or by throwing it into the fire. But Gandalf tells him that it can only be destroyed in the volcano where it was made, in the Crack of Doom in Mordor. This information scares Frodo, and he doubts he'll be able to perform such a deed. But for now he accepts the responsibility of guarding the Ring and will take it to Rivendell, where it will be out of Sauron's grasp.

At this point, Sam Gamgee, the gardener, is discovered eavesdropping. He shows even less comprehension of the situation than Frodo does. When told he can accompany Frodo, Sam is overjoyed: "Me go and see Elves and all! Hooray!"

When Frodo at last leaves the Shire, he is accompanied by one of his friends, Peregrine Took (Pippin), and by Sam Gamgee. Gandalf was to go with them but hasn't been heard from in several months.

This part of the story is filled with vivid descriptions of the pleasures of the road: crackling fires, amiable conversation, and, most of all, the landscape—trees, fields, and stars. The richness of detail, while adding little to the plot, is an important part of Tolkien's style. Many readers find that these descriptions make Middle-earth and its inhabitants come alive.

The travelers soon find they are being pursued by mysterious Black Riders. Twice they are forced to hide in the woods as a Rider approaches. Both times they are nearly discovered, and both times Frodo is seized with an almost irresistible desire to put on the Ring. The first time, for an inexplicable reason, the Rider turns away. The second Rider is driven off by the voices of elves, who then offer the hobbits protection for the night.

NOTE: The Black Riders give the impression of silent menace. They wear black cloaks and hoods; not even their faces can be seen. They track the hobbits through a sense of smell, making them seem animalistic.

The elven leader warns Frodo that the Riders are deadly "servants of the Enemy."

In the morning the three hobbits start out, closely pursued by Black Riders. They safely reach the house Frodo had bought to hide the fact he was planning to leave the Shire. There Frodo is joined by Meriadoc Brandybuck (Merry) and Fatty Bolger. Fatty will stay behind to keep up the pretense that Frodo is living there, but Merry and Pippin insist on going with Frodo, no matter how great the danger. Frodo has been told by both Gandalf and the elves that he should rely on the help of friends. Though he doesn't want to bring them into danger, he's happy to know they'll come. Through Merry, Pippin, and Sam, Tolkien is expressing the importance of friendship.

The hobbits decide not to take the road, which is likely to be watched by Black Riders. Instead they try to cut through the Old Forest. It's a weird place, and it's said that the trees can move, hemming in unwelcome strangers. The hobbits are soon lost and find themselves on the bank of the River Withywindle, in the heart of the forest.

They are sitting in the shade of an old willow when suddenly Merry and Pippin are swallowed up by great cracks in the tree. Frodo's cries for help are answered by Tom Bombadil, a strange old man with a feathered hat. Tom soon forces Old Man Willow to release his captives; then he invites them to his home. Tom tells the hobbits that they were lucky he came by, for he did not actually hear their cries: "Just chance brought me . . . if chance you call it." Many readers interpret this as a hint of some unseen power that guided Tom to come along at that moment and save the hobbits.

BOOK I, CHAPTERS 7–12

The hobbits are safely sent on their way again by Tom. They are joined by a mysterious character named Strider, who guides them to Rivendell.

*

The hobbits meet Tom's beautiful wife, Goldberry, the daughter of the River Withywindle. Tom and Goldberry are curious yet appealing figures.

Tom often speaks in song; even when he isn't singing, his words have a singsong quality. His love
for Goldberry is touching, and when the hobbits
first meet him, he is bringing lilies to place in bowls
around her feet. There seems to be good magic in
Tom and Goldberry's home, for Tom says that no
evil can touch the hobbits there. Not even the Ring
has power over Tom. When he puts it on, he remains visible, and when Frodo puts it on, Tom can
still see him.

NOTE: Tom and Goldberry as Nature Spirits   Tom
and Goldberry may be seen as nature spirits, figures who represent the forces of nature—for example, Mother Nature. Another example is Pan,
the Greek god of the woodlands, who was half
man and half goat. Pan was believed to be mischievous and fun-loving, but also dangerous when
angry. He belonged to the world of nature and
seldom concerned himself with human affairs.
Traces of Pan can be seen in Tom Bombadil, with
his humorous appearance (although Tom is fully
human), his lively personality, and his power over
nature.

Goldberry tells the hobbits that Tom is the master of wood, water, and hill. Tom's songs, such as
the one he uses to make Old Man Willow release
Pippin and Merry, seem to give him power over
nature. Goldberry shares in this power, for her
song brings rain. "This is Goldberry's washing day,"
Tom tells the hobbits.

People who think Tom is a nature spirit say that
this is why the Ring has no influence on him. The

Ring is of the world of man, and Tom is of the world of nature. He is untouched by the desire for absolute power that the Ring represents.

The hobbits set off across the barrow-downs, a stretch of land that is filled with burial mounds, or barrows. Foolishly lingering there until sundown, against Tom's advice, they become lost in fog and are captured by a barrow-wight (an evil spirit who inhabits these burial mounds and lures travelers to their death). Frodo sings the rhymed call for help that Tom Bombadil had taught them, and soon Tom arrives to rescue them.

While in the barrow, Frodo has again been tempted to put on the Ring. You can see how Tolkien's treatment of the Ring has changed from *The Hobbit*. In that book Bilbo often used the Ring to save his friends. Now the Ring serves only as a temptation to Frodo to take the easy way out and abandon his friends. This is a moment of truth for Frodo and relates to Tolkien's theme of the corrupting effect of power. Frodo must choose between using the Ring to save himself or facing certain death but not compromising his morals. This hints at another of Tolkien's themes—refusal to give in to despair. Frodo fights, even with no hope of winning, and finds a way to rescue his friends. The importance of friendship also comes into play here, for it is Frodo's friendship for the others that keeps him from putting on the Ring and falling into evil.

Tom gives each of the hobbits a sword from the barrow. They feel awkward wearing them, for they had never thought of fighting. This is an idea they'll

have to get used to, however, if they are to survive. The swords are a sign that the hobbits must
start learning to take responsibility for themselves.

NOTE: The Power of Language   Tom Bombadil
uses song to drive the wight from the barrow, just
as he used it to force Old Man Willow to release
Merry and Pippin. He also gives names to the hobbits' ponies. There is an ancient belief, held by
many primitive people, that everything has its own
name, in a secret language. Knowing the name
gives you power over the thing (or person). It seems
that Tom's mastery over things comes from the
power to name them. By giving Tom this power,
Tolkien introduces a new perspective on language.
Throughout the book you will see that Tolkien
draws attention to language in different ways.

The hobbits safely reach their next destination,
the town of Bree, and stay at an inn, the Prancing
Pony. Frodo foolishly allows the Ring to slip onto
his finger. By disappearing, he reveals his identity
to the watching spies. He is rebuked by a mysterious character called Strider, who knows Frodo's
name and also seems to know about the Ring. Strider offers to join the hobbits as their guide. After
initial distrust, they decide to accept. They're start-
ing to be aware that they've been too careless, and
someone with Strider's experience will be able to
help them.

To stay off the road, Strider leads the hobbits
along a twisting course through the forest, arriving
one night at a hill called Weathertop. So far there

has been no sign of the Black Riders, but that night on Weathertop the hobbits are attacked.

Strider has said that the Riders cannot see the world of light; they see best in darkness. This is appropriate, for light symbolizes good, and darkness evil. When Frodo puts on the Ring, the Riders seem suddenly to see him. And Frodo finds that he can now see their faces and armor, whereas before they were only shadowy figures. It seems he has entered the Riders' world by putting on the Ring. Suddenly, one of the Riders attacks Frodo and succeeds in stabbing him before being driven off.

When Frodo regains consciousness, he learns from the others that they had seen little of his encounter with the Black Rider. Frodo had seemed to vanish, and the Rider appeared only as a black shadow rushing past them. Strider now tends Frodo's wound. The Black Rider's knife has deadly magic in it, and already a chill is spreading from Frodo's shoulder down his arm and side. Strider says that the evil of that knife is beyond his skill to cure, so they all set out for Rivendell, hoping that there Frodo can be healed.

On the way they are joined by an Elf-lord, Glorfindel, who has been sent from Rivendell by Elrond to find the travelers and help them. Glorfindel gives Frodo his own horse, which can outrun the steeds of the Black Riders. When the company reaches a ford in the river, the Black Riders suddenly appear, and Glorfindel sends his horse, with Frodo on it, over the ford. Calling on Frodo to wait, the Black Riders start to follow him. He no longer has the strength to refuse. Still, he resists their hold to the last, calling out defiantly. They only laugh and advance confidently to take him. Suddenly the river floods, and on the other shore a shining figure, Glorfindel, can be seen driving the Riders into the water. The last thing Frodo sees is the Riders and their black horses being carried away by the river.

BOOK II, CHAPTERS 1–5

A fellowship is formed to accompany Frodo south toward Mordor. They pass through the mines of Moria, where Gandalf is lost in battle with a Balrog.

*

Frodo awakens in Rivendell to find the wizard sitting by his bed. He learns from Gandalf about the Black Riders and the events at the ford. The Black Riders, Gandalf tells Frodo, are the nine ringwraiths, men who have been enslaved by Sauron through rings of power. Frodo had very nearly fallen into their power. If he had not reached Rivendell in time, the power of the Rider's knife would have turned him into a wraith, under the dominion of Sauron.

Chapter 1 contains a great deal of information, revealed mostly through dialogue. Frodo learns from Gandalf about the nature of the elves. The elves had at one time lived in the Blessed Realm, which lies beyond the western sea. They now live in both worlds and have power over both the seen and unseen. (Later, Tolkien slips in the information that the elves are immortal.) Gandalf tells Frodo that there is great power in Rivendell to withstand Sauron. He also comments that there is power of another kind in the Shire. Can you guess what that power is? This is an important question to keep in mind as you read the book.

NOTE: Tolkien's Christianity   Tolkien was a devout Christian, and some people read *The Lord of the Rings* as a Christian allegory. In chapter 1 you can see why. Frodo learns that the gleaming figure he saw by the ford was Glorfindel, appearing in the form that he assumes "on the other side" (presumably in the unseen world, though perhaps Gandalf is referring to the Blessed Realm). Glorfindel sounds almost like an angel, and in fact, some readers believe that the elves are angels and that the Blessed Realm is heaven. Tolkien, however, strongly denied that his books are allegorical. An example of a work intended as Christian allegory is *Pilgrim's Progress* by John Bunyan (1678). In that book the characters journey through an imaginary landscape toward heaven. Their journey is the journey of life, or of faith, and their adventures represent the pitfalls on the way to salvation, such as despair and greed. Tolkien is quoted as having said that he never intended to have his book interpreted in such a manner. However, he admitted that while religion is never mentioned in *The Lord of the Rings* (in fact, he deliberately deleted references to religion), the principles of his faith are deeply imbedded in the story. Gandalf's statement that Frodo was chosen to bear the Ring hints at the workings of divine providence. Frodo is tempted by evil when he feels compelled to put on the Ring. Be alert to these religious undertones as you read the book.

A great feast is held in Frodo's honor. There, Gandalf, Elrond, and Glorfindel appear as awe-inspiring figures, a change from *The Hobbit*, where characters are often made fun of. After the feast, Frodo finds Bilbo in a large hall where the elves now gather to sing and talk.

One small event casts a pall on the evening. When Bilbo asks to see the Ring and Frodo shows it to him, it is as if a shadow suddenly falls between the two hobbits. (Note again Tolkien's use of shadow as a symbol for evil.) Frodo sees Bilbo as a wrinkled, grasping creature and feels an urge to hit him. Around them, the singing of the elves falters, and there is sudden silence. Bilbo realizes that the Ring has already affected Frodo's personality.

Strider is also revealed as an awe-inspiring figure, one of the few remaining descendants of a great and ancient race of men, the Númenórea. Strider's true name is Aragorn; to show his new status in the book, he is called by that name, instead of Strider.

Notice the star imagery in chapter 1. In Elrond's eyes is a light like the light of stars. Bilbo twice refers to stars: first in his song about Eärendil, who is turned into a star, and at the end of the chapter, when he says he will go to look at the stars of Elbereth. (Elbereth is a being from the Blessed Realm who is believed by the elves to have created the stars.) Aragorn appears to Frodo as having a star shining on his breast. Whereas shadow is a symbol of evil, stars emerge in Tolkien's book as a symbol of a distant, yet enduring good.

A council is held at Rivendell, and all races—dwarves, elves, men, and hobbits—are represented.

Ostensibly they have come to bring news and to seek advice. Yet Elrond says that they have been brought here by some higher purpose. The stories they have to tell all relate in some way to the rise of Sauron, as well as to the Ring, which Frodo now carries.

Elrond's story of the Ring encompasses a broad sweep of history, for he has lived through three ages and seen evil rise and fall many times. Next, Boromir, a man from the country of Gondor to the south, tells of Sauron's rise in Mordor. The forces of Gondor are trying to hold back the tide of evil, but they're too weak against Sauron's might.

Aragorn chooses this moment to reveal that he's the heir of Elendil, once king of Gondor, who had been slain in the last battle against Sauron many years ago. He has Elendil's broken sword, and the time has come for that sword to be reforged and for Aragorn to return to Gondor as rightful king.

NOTE: Elements of Elitism in *The Lord of the Rings*
The passage where Aragorn describes his life as a Ranger shows the elitism that people see in *The Lord of the Rings*. Aragorn's words depict an elite few who spend their lives facing danger and discomfort for the sake of the many, who are simple and weak. The Rangers are scorned for their trouble, while the simple folk remain blissfully ignorant of the dangers they are being protected from. Aragorn considers it right that things should be this way. Do you agree with his theory? Is it better for the common people to be kept unaware of the

dangers in the world? Do you know of governments and leaders who seem to feel that way?

Gandalf has the worst news of all. His tale is of the treachery of Saruman the White, a wizard like Gandalf, and head of the council that drove Sauron from Mirkwood. Secretly Saruman has for some time desired the Ring for himself, and when he suspects that Gandalf knows where it is, he summons him under the pretext of offering help against the Black Riders and Sauron. But instead he tells Gandalf that they must join forces and use the power of the Ring to rule Middle-earth. While certain evils would have to be tolerated and weaker allies cast aside, Saruman claims it would all serve a higher good. When Gandalf refuses to join him, Saruman imprisons him on the top of a mountain. Gandalf is finally rescued by Gwaihir, the eagle.

The council must now decide what is to be done with the Ring. Boromir suggests they use the Ring's power against Sauron. Elrond explains that whoever used the Ring to defeat Sauron, no matter how noble his purpose, would become just as evil as Sauron, for such is the nature of the Ring. The very desire for the Ring corrupts the heart, as it corrupted Saruman.

NOTE: Nature of Good and Evil   In this scene you will find many of Tolkien's ideas about good and evil. Nothing ever starts out evil—even Sauron was good once. Elrond's experience has shown him that evil can never be completely vanquished, for it always reappears in a new form. And even the temporary victories of good over evil are won only at great cost. Yet despite its power, evil has a weakness in that it cannot imagine good—for example, Sauron thinks that all people desire power as he does, and so he does not expect them to destroy the Ring.

The power of good can be seen in the three rings that the elves possess. Elrond said that the elven rings were not made to obtain wealth or dominion over others, but were made to be used for healing, understanding, and creating. This more passive kind of power is an alternative to Sauron's (and Saruman's) desire to control the world. However, the fate of the elven rings is tied up with the fate of the Ruling Ring. If Sauron should regain possession of his Ring, he will be able to control the elven rings. If the Ring is destroyed, Elrond believes that the power of the elven rings will end, and many good and beautiful things will pass from Middle-earth. This is another example of Tolkien's theme that the forces of good achieve victory only at great cost to themselves. It also presents another facet of Tolkien's complex theme of the relationship between good and evil; often evil purpose can unintentionally bring about beneficial results. In this case, the elven rings were forged at Sauron's direction, to win control over elves. Instead the rings have brought about much good and are invaluable in the struggle against him.

Not everyone accepts the fact that the Ring must be destroyed. Some feel that to bring the Ring to Mordor would be an act of despair or folly. But

Gandalf says that it's the only possible path. It must be taken even if it seems doomed to failure. Elrond suggests that this quest may be undertaken by the weak as well as the strong, for neither strength nor wisdom will insure success. Here Tolkien stresses his theme of the power of the common man: "Yet such is oft the course of deeds that move the wheels of the world: small hands do them because they must, while the eyes of the great are elsewhere." Frodo agrees to take on the task of destroying the Ring, something that until now he had hoped to leave to someone else. Elrond says that he believes Frodo was chosen for this task and that only he can succeed. Yet it's important that he accepts the task of his own free will. With this, Tolkien brings up the last of his major themes, that of free will. While destiny seems to play a hand in the lives of Tolkien's characters, they are free to refuse that destiny, just as Frodo is free to refuse to be Ring-bearer.

Elrond chooses eight companions for Frodo: Gandalf, Aragorn, Gimli the dwarf, Legolas the elf, Boromir, Sam, Merry, and Pippin.

Aragorn's broken sword is reforged, and he re-names it Anduril. In place of Frodo's broken sword Bilbo offers him his own sword Sting. In this scene between the two hobbits, Tolkien suggests a comparison with legendary heroes, such as King Arthur, who draw a sword from a stone or tree where it has been imbedded for many years. Here, Bilbo thrusts Sting into a beam and Frodo draws it out. *The Lord of the Rings* has many such allusions, which, while not crucial to an understanding of the story, add richness to Tolkien's work.

The company plans to cross the Misty Moun-

tains through the Redhorn Gate, but a sudden bliz-
zard forces them to turn back. It seems to have
been directed against them on purpose, but Gandalf does not believe that Sauron was responsible.
Rather, he feels that the mountain itself, hostile
toward travelers, sought to stop them. This serves
as a reminder, in Tolkien's philosophy, that there
are neutral forces at work that serve neither good
nor evil.

Gandalf leads the company through the mines
of Moria, once the home of dwarves, but now inhabited by orcs (Tolkien called them goblins in *The
Hobbit*) and other evil creatures. Pippin impul-
sively throws a pebble down a well, angering Gandalf, for it may alert the orcs to their presence in
the mines. Later they are attacked by orcs and trolls,
and even Sam and Frodo have a chance to prove
their courage. For the most part, however, the four
hobbits must be protected and herded about like
children as the company flees through the mines
toward the Great Gate. They reach the bridge of
Khazad-dûm, which arches over a deep chasm.
Beyond the bridge lies the Great Gate. At that moment a Balrog (a terrifying creature from the mines
of Moria) appears among their pursuers. Gandalf
sends the others forward, and on the bridge itself
he turns to meet the Balrog.

In the confrontation you can see how Tolkien
uses his imagery of light and shadow, contrasting
the light of Gandalf's sword with the vast shadow
surrounding the Balrog. Before the Balrog, Gandalf seems small and frail, as good always does
before evil in *The Lord of the Rings*. But appearances
can be deceiving, and Gandalf succeeds in break-
ing the Balrog's sword. As he casts the Balrog into

the chasm, the creature's whip wraps around the wizard's leg. The others watch in horror as Gandalf also plunges into the chasm. Then they quickly flee to the Great Gate and out into the safety of the sunlight. There they stop to mourn the loss of Gandalf.

BOOK II, CHAPTERS 6–10

The band enjoys an interlude in the beautiful forest of Lothlórien. They then continue south, where disaster awaits them.

*

The company enters the forest of Lothlórien, the home of elves. Boromir has heard rumors that this is a perilous place and doesn't want to enter. But Aragorn and Legolas know of Lothlórien as a place of power that thwarts evil. Like Rivendell, it is a refuge from the darkness in the land. At first the travelers are met with suspicion by the elves. In such dangerous times the elves can trust no strangers.

In Lothlórien (also called Lórien), Frodo feels as though he has entered the world of the Elder days, where the ancient past is still alive. Lothlórien seems to him to be a timeless land that will neither fade nor change. In the wind he hears the sounds of waves and seabirds from the distant past.

The company meets Galadriel and Celeborn, the rulers of Lothlórien. Galadriel describes how she and her husband have struggled against evil through the ages. She speaks of the struggle as the long defeat. She tests the members of the fellowship in turn, silently offering them the choice of going on into danger or turning aside and having the one thing they most desire. As they talk of it later, Boromir holds that Galadriel was tempting them and warns that she is a danger. Of all the company, he alone fails to recognize the goodness in Lórien.

NOTE: Tolkien and Women   Tolkien has often been criticized for generally ignoring women in his books. There may be merit in this argument. Think back to *The Hobbit:* The only female character was Lobelia Sackville-Baggins, a ridiculous and unpleasant hobbit. In *The Lord of the Rings* thus far, you have met only Lobelia, Goldberry, Arwen (Elrond's daughter), and now Galadriel. Galadriel is a figure of great power. She seems wiser than her husband, Celeborn, and wins over Gimli the dwarf with her kindness. She is the one who first called together the White Council that originally drove Sauron from Mirkwood. She's also the possessor of one of the three elven rings. Equal even to Sauron's power, she can read his thoughts, yet he can't find her.

Galadriel, however, represents an idealized woman, as do Arwen and Goldberry. Later in the trilogy, you will meet a contrast in the character of Éowyn.

In Lothlórien you can clearly see the way Tolkien equates nature with beneficent power. Lothlórien is a place of great natural beauty. The elves, who make their houses in the trees, are in close contact with nature, leading a simple life-style without technology. Sam says that he can't tell if the elves made the land or the land made them, proving that he can be surprisingly perceptive at times. The magic in Lothlórien is well hidden, yet it is pervasive and powerful.

Galadriel offers Sam and Frodo a look in her "mirror," a basin of water. In it, Sam sees visions of him and Frodo, then of the Shire. He sees trees being cut down and ugly buildings with smoking chimneys being built. He wants to return to the Shire at once, but Galadriel warns that the mirror can be deceptive.

Frodo sees in the mirror the great red eye of Sauron, which he feels is seeking him. Galadriel tells him not to fear while he's in Lothlórien, for Sauron's eye cannot find him there, although she herself can read Sauron's thoughts. This echoes what another elf had said in a previous chapter: though the light pierces the very heart of darkness, the light's own secret has not yet been discovered. Galadriel reveals to Frodo that secret: she possesses one of the elven rings. It appears as a star upon her hand. If you have any doubts about Galadriel's motives, this should answer them, for stars, as you know by now, are Tolkien's symbol for good.

Galadriel's fate, and the fate of Lothlórien, are in Frodo's hands. If Frodo should fail, Lothlórien will be laid bare to Sauron. If Frodo succeeds and the One Ring is destroyed, Galadriel's power will diminish and Lórien will fade. Either way, it seems that Lothlórien is doomed. Frodo offers the Ring to Galadriel, but she refuses it, saying that if she used it against Sauron, she would become as terrible as him. Galadriel seems to swell in size, showing Frodo what she would be like if she possessed the Ring. Then she again becomes a simply clad elf-woman. "I pass the test," she tells him. "I will diminish and go into the West and remain Galadriel."

The travelers now must decide whether they will travel along the east side of the river toward Mordor or take the western bank and go from there to Minas Tirith, Boromir's city. Boromir reveals that he still believes that the Ring should be used against Sauron, and that it's folly to take it into Mordor. The decision is postponed when Celeborn offers to give them boats, so that they can travel down the river many miles before having to choose their course. The elves also provide *lembas*—thin, nourishing cakes—and cloaks that have the power of invisibility. *Lembas* and the waterlike drink of the elves that has appeared throughout the book are interpreted as communion wafers and holy water by some. But behind the specifically Christian symbolism of bread and water is a recognition of the power in such basic necessities of life, a recognition shared by many other people and religions. Tolkien himself said that he wanted to present things in a new light, to give people a sense of wonder at the ordinary. This may be the inspiration behind *lembas* and the miraculous drink of the elves, rather than a deliberate allusion to Christianity.

NOTE: Elves in Lore and Literature   The word *elf* seems to have originated in Norse mythology and to have been carried over into English as another name for fairy. Many people think of elves as fairies such as Tinkerbell in *Peter Pan* or those in Shakespeare's play *A Midsummer Night's Dream*. Tolkien often expressed his dislike for these diminutive fairies, who ride insects and live in flowers. His elves present a different picture. While they are given to joyous feasting, they are also a race of stern warriors. This change represents a step backward in time, from modern-day fairy tales and the literary fancies of Shakespeare's day to the medieval romances that Tolkien's works are often compared to. In these romances fairies are beautiful and powerful creatures who are equal in size to humans, who can be hostile toward mortals, and who engage in hunts and warfare, as Tolkien's elves do.

These fairies, in turn, represent the dwindled gods of pagan mythologies. The Irish fairies, the Daoine Sidhe, are the last of the old gods, the Tuatha Da Danaan, who left Ireland for their homeland across the sea, Tir Nan Og or The Land of the Young. In *The Lord of the Rings*, the most powerful elves, such as Galadriel, take on this godlike stature. Like the Tuatha Da Danaan, the Tolkien elves are slowly leaving Middle-earth, passing over the sea to their homeland in the Blessed Realm.

Many characteristics of the elves in *The Lord of the Rings* are shared by fairies of lore and legend. Like Tolkien's elves, fairies are immortal. They're associated with weaving and with the bestowing of gifts, such as Galadriel gives to the company. But the Tolkien elves differ in one important way.

Belief in fairies had dwindled along with paganism as the influence of Christianity grew in Europe. Fairies were often depicted as amoral and came to represent a way of life opposite to the good life of the Christian faith. Tolkien ennobles his elves by allying them with the good and making them the most ethical of his races.

The company travels down the river until they reach the point at which they must choose between Minas Tirith and Mordor. Frodo, as Ringbearer, must decide his course, and the others will follow him or not as they choose. Frodo goes off alone to think, and after a time Boromir joins him. Boromir, who has been acting strangely, tries to convince Frodo to give him the Ring, so that he can use its power against the enemy. When Frodo refuses, he tries to take it. Frodo puts on the Ring and disappears. As he runs away, he feels the eye of Sauron searching for him.

In this scene Tolkien shows the relationship between destiny and free will. Two voices struggle within Frodo. One is that of Sauron, calling Frodo to him. The other tells Frodo to take off the Ring. Suddenly realizing that he's free to choose, he takes off the Ring. Already he's seen the evil power of the Ring at work in its temptation of Boromir. Therefore, he decides to pursue the quest alone. He tries to slip away by boat but Sam catches up with him. Together, the two hobbits head for Mordor.

PART TWO: THE TWO TOWERS

BOOK III, CHAPTERS 1–5

Aragorn, Legolas, and Gimli set out to rescue Merry and Pippin, who have been captured by orcs (referred to as goblins in *The Hobbit*).

*

Orcs attack while the rest of the fellowship is still scattered, searching for Frodo. Boromir is mortally wounded as he defends Merry and Pippin, who are bound and carried away by the orcs. Before he dies, Boromir tells Aragorn that he tried to take the Ring from Frodo. But instead of criticizing him, Aragorn praises his bravery in defending the hobbits. Boromir is given a hero's funeral by Aragorn, Legolas, and Gimli. Like Thorin Oakenshield in *The Hobbit,* Boromir has made up for his evil deeds through an act of great valor.

Aragorn faces a dilemma: should he follow Frodo into Mordor, or try to save Merry and Pippin? Have you ever had to make a choice between doing what you *thought* you should do, and doing what you *felt* you had to do? This is Aragorn's dilemma. He chooses to follow his feelings and try to rescue his friends. (Although Sam and Frodo are his friends too, they have chosen to go on alone, and Aragorn decides to respect that choice.) Do you think Aragorn made the right choice? Why?

As Aragorn, Legolas, and Gimli follow the trail of the orcs, they are heartened at the discovery of hobbit prints and a fallen clasp from Pippin's cloak. They meet a troop of horsemen led by Éomer, a marshal of Rohan, and learn from him that the orcs they were tracking have all been killed by the men of Rohan, but that the hobbits weren't seen. Éomer agrees to lend the three companions some horses so that they might continue their seemingly hopeless quest.

The next two chapters return to the scene when Merry and Pippin were captured by the orcs. The orcs are actually from three different places and

constantly fight among themselves. It is characteristic of Tolkien's evil creatures that they cannot
cooperate. The orcs from the mines of Moria in the
Misty Mountains are seeking vengeance. Sauron's
orcs want to take the hobbits back to Mordor. The
strongest band, Saruman's orcs, have orders to take
the hobbits to their master in Isengard. Fortunately, the orcs are intercepted by the men of Rohan, and during the ensuing battle Merry and Pippin manage to slip away. They hide in the forest
of Fangorn, where they meet Treebeard, an Ent.

Ents are another of Tolkien's creations that have
captured the imagination of readers. Like Tom
Bombadil, they are part of the natural world and
show the power of nature. They are shepherds of
trees and look like trees themselves. Their chief is
Treebeard. Some people call him Fangorn, which
is also the name of the forest. He is very ancient,
the oldest living thing still to walk the earth. When
Merry and Pippin tell him their story, Treebeard
realizes that Saruman is trying to make himself
into a rival power to Sauron. Treebeard decides
that Saruman must be stopped, but not because of
the danger he poses to the people of Gondor and
Rohan. (Nor does Treebeard take sides in the battle against Sauron. This is consistent with the idea
that nature is neutral in the struggle between good
and evil.) He bases his decision on the fact that
Saruman's orcs have been cutting down trees on
the edge of Fangorn, leaving the land desolate.
(This wanton destruction of nature is an important
sign of evil in Tolkien's world.)

The Ents, like the forces of good, believe in the
importance of free will. They're very independent
and can't be forced to do something they don't want
to do. Treebeard can only lead by convincing them

he is right. After a lengthy council meeting, they decide to march on Isengard, to stop Saruman.

The story at this point returns to Aragorn, Legolas, and Gimli. In the forest they meet Gandalf, who tells them that Merry and Pippin are in safe hands. They learn from the wizard how he fought with the Balrog after his fall and at last overcame him. Gandalf passed through fire and death and emerged renewed. He is no longer Gandalf the Grey, but Gandalf the White, taking Saruman's place.

Gandalf points out that there is a purpose at work in the world. If Merry and Pippin hadn't come on the quest, they would not have been there for Boromir to protect. Their presence saved Boromir by giving him an opportunity for redemption through sacrificing himself for the sake of others. Gandalf also points out how the work of evil can be turned to good purpose: The orcs' capture of Merry and Pippin resulted in the arrival of the hobbits in Fangorn Forest just in time to arouse the Ents against Saruman.

BOOK III, CHAPTERS 6–11

Satisfied that Merry and Pippin are safe, Aragorn, Legolas, and Gimli join the men of Rohan in battle against the evil wizard Saruman.

*

Aragorn, Legolas, and Gimli now ride with Gandalf to Edoras, the palace of Théoden, king of Rohan.

NOTE: Rohan is also called the Mark of Rohan and the Riddermark, and the Riders of Rohan are

sometimes referred to as the Rohirrim and the Riders
of the Mark. They are warriors, and Gandalf says
of them that they are unlearned but wise. Many
readers have commented on their similarity to the
Anglo-Saxons, the ancestors of the English. The
most important difference between the men of Rohan and the Anglo-Saxons is that the Anglo-Saxons didn't have the Rohirrims' love for horses. Other
than that, the two cultures are very similar. The
language of Rohan is based on Anglo-Saxon. The
song of Rohan that Aragorn sings in chapter 6 is
modeled after a famous Anglo-Saxon poem, *The
Wanderer*. This poem talks about how fleeting life
is and how with time all traces of a man's life are
erased. The Anglo-Saxons reacted to this awareness—as did the ancient Greeks in *The Iliad* and
The Odyssey—by seeking glory so that their names
would be remembered in song. The men of Rohan
also show this awareness of death and desire for
glory. And because they accept death as inevita-
ble, they also accept the idea that it's not whether
you win or lose that matters, but whether you act
rightly. Thus, in their view, it's better to choose a
noble death than to survive and compromise yourself. The courage of the Riders is an illustration of
Tolkien's theme of heroism.

Gandalf and the others are at first met with suspicion in Edoras. At one point an argument breaks
out when Aragorn refuses to leave his sword outside the king's hall. Gandalf gently reminds him
that they're all friends—or at least should be; only
Mordor will benefit if they quarrel. Aragorn reluctantly leaves his sword. In doing so, he's learned

that sometimes he must swallow his pride in the interest of peace.

After Gandalf frees Théoden from the influence of his evil councilor, Gríma the Wormtongue, the king agrees to do battle with Saruman. In Gríma, a spy for Saruman, you can see Tolkien's ideas about evil. You are told that Gríma wasn't always evil but was corrupted by Saruman. Given the opportunity to redeem himself, he refuses, but even so is treated with mercy. To kill or imprison him would itself be evil, and so could bring forth no good.

Notice the style of the writing. The sentence structure, or syntax, is very formal, as in "Never again shall it be said, Gandalf, that you come only with grief." Tolkien also uses old-fashioned words, such as *hearken* and *behold*, to help establish the mood and to add the flavor of ancient epics.

For the first time Aragorn meets Éowyn, Théoden's niece. She is very beautiful, but also appears to Aragorn to be cold, not yet come to womanhood. Éowyn sees in him a man of great power and seems to be falling in love with him. He reacts by acting troubled. As the army rides out, Éowyn stays behind to watch over her people. She wears mail and carries a sword like a warrior. Keep all of this in mind, for Éowyn will later play an important role in the story.

Théoden's army appears to have ridden to certain defeat. They hold the great fortress of Helm's Deep against Saruman's forces, but can't resist the foes' onslaughts much longer. Rather than give in to despair, Théoden and his men ride out in a last desperate attack. But the tide of battle is reversed when Gandalf arrives with reinforcements, and the orcs are driven into a mysterious and frightening forest that has appeared overnight around Helm's Deep. As the victorious forces set out for Isengard, Saruman's stronghold, they learn from Gandalf that the army of trees has been led here by the Ents.

At Isengard, the king and his company find Merry and Pippin relaxing in front of the shattered gates. The hobbits tell how the Ents, led by Treebeard, attacked Isengard and overthrew Saruman.

Gandalf speaks with Saruman, who is holed up in the tower of Orthanc with the traitor Gríma. Gandalf offers Saruman an opportunity to repent and join the side of good, but Saruman scornfully refuses. Gandalf then breaks Saruman's staff, casting him out of the order of wizards and out of the White Council. Now a weak, pitiable figure, Saruman is sentenced to be kept prisoner in his tower, guarded by the Ents.

At the same moment that Gandalf breaks Saruman's staff, Gríma angrily throws a heavy round stone at Gandalf but misses him. It is a *palantír*, a stone of seeing, perhaps the greatest treasure that Saruman had. Once again, evil intent has a good effect, for the stone is very valuable.

Pippin is drawn to the stone and sneaks a look into it later that night. Sauron appears in a vision and questions him, believing that Pippin is Saruman's prisoner. Sauron calls Pippin "it" and speaks of him as a dainty morsel, an object rather than an individual. It was amusing in *The Hobbit* when Gollum called Bilbo "it." But now this peculiarity of speech takes on evil significance. It shows Sauron's possessiveness and his denial of the individuality and free will of others.

Galfand presents the *palantír* to Aragorn, to whom

it belongs as rightful heir to the throne of Gondor. As they speak, a Nazgûl, one of the ringwraiths, passes overhead on his winged steed. It is a sign that war will come soon. Taking Pippin with him, Gandalf rides at once for Gondor, which will be the first country to be attacked.

BOOK IV, CHAPTERS 1–5

Frodo and Sam begin the tortuous journey to Mordor, guided by Gollum. They meet Faramir, a captain of Gondor's army, who is stationed just outside Mordor.

*

On their journey to Mordor, Frodo and Sam capture Gollum, who has been following them since the company passed through the mines of Moria. Frodo remembers his conversation with Gandalf long ago, when he told the wizard that Bilbo should have killed Gollum. But now that Frodo has the opportunity, he doesn't kill Gollum either. Why not?

There's a change in Gollum's voice and language when he seems to relive for a moment the torment he endured in Mordor, and laments the loss of his precious Ring. This is the first glimpse Tolkien gives you of another side of Gollum's personality. He reveals a soul in torment, struggling with itself. But the evil self is still stronger, and Gollum reverts to his usual manner of speaking.

Frodo makes Gollum swear to obey him and to lead them into Mordor. As if in a vision, Sam sees a physical change in Frodo, who appears for a moment like a mighty lord, with Gollum a whining dog at his feet. After swearing to obey Frodo, Gollum now starts speaking normally again, and calls himself Sméagol, the name he had before he found the Ring. Although he acts fearful, he's also pitifully eager to please and appears insanely happy whenever Frodo is kind to him. What do you think has caused this change in him? If you pay close attention to Gollum's speech in the next few chapters, you will find that it gives clues to the struggle going on inside him.

Gollum guides the hobbits through the Dead Marshes. They travel in darkness, and all around them they see what seem to be candles burning. The marsh is the scene of an ancient battle, and in the water the hobbits glimpse the faces of the long dead, both good folks and evil. The lights are actually based on fact; they are caused by gasses that escape the rotting muck of the marsh floor and spontaneously ignite. In folktales they are called candles of the dead or will-o'-the-wisps and are believed to lead travelers astray. Tolkien uses this folk belief to create a nightmarish landscape.

They next pass through another nightmarish landscape, worse than the marshes. The land around Mordor is desolate. Saruman's crime of cutting down trees pales next to what Sauron has done. Tolkien's descriptions are powerful: "The gasping pools were choked with ash and crawling muds, sickly white and grey, as if the mountains had vomited the filth of their entrails upon the lands." Nothing lives there, "not even the leprous growths that feed on rottenness." This is a land that has been defiled beyond healing, and it shows not only the depth of Sauron's power but also the depth of his evil.

Tolkien's description of the desolation outside

Mordor is reminiscent of modern wastelands caused by industries and strip mining: it is filled with mounds of poison-stained earth, gaping pits, and noxious fumes. Many readers believe that Tolkien is intentionally making a comment on the destruction of nature by technology. Remember that *The Lord of the Rings* was written more than thirty years ago. Seeing all the attention that the harmful effects of industry and pollution are now getting, we can acknowledge that Tolkien was ahead of his time.

NOTE: Wastelands in Literature   Wastelands are often used in literature as a symbol of spiritual barrenness. Two good examples of this occur in F. Scott Fitzgerald's *The Great Gatsby* (1925) and T. S. Eliot's famous poem, *The Waste Land* (1922). In *The Great Gatsby*, Nick, the narrator, passes through a wasteland of ashes on his way into New York City. In T. S. Eliot's poem there is no wasteland except in the title, which serves as a metaphor for the lives described in the poem. In both, the wasteland is interpreted as a symbol for the sterility of modern life: the ugliness of the city, the lack of caring relationships, and the lack of any sense of purpose. It's likely that Tolkien was aware of this tradition and either consciously or unconsciously drew on it when he described the wastes around Mordor. How does the wasteland as a symbol of *inner* barrenness relate to Tolkien's concept of evil?

Meanwhile, the struggle between the two sides

of Gollum's personality continues. One day, while Sam is pretending to sleep, he overhears Gollum debating with himself. As Sméagol, he wants to keep his promise to Frodo; as Gollum, he wants to take the Ring for himself. The Gollum side decides to wait for the aid of a mysterious "She." This idea terrifies the Sméagol personality.

Frodo had originally intended to try to find a way in through the Black Gate of Mordor. It seems to be an impossible feat. But he resolves to attempt it, because his task is to go into Mordor and he knows of no other way. (If you look at the map in the book, you will see that Mordor is surrounded by mountains on all but the eastern border, which is furthest from the Black Gate.) Sam is dismayed, but loyally resolves to follow his master anywhere.

Gollum is wild with fear. He's all too familiar with Sauron's power and what it would mean for Sauron to regain possession of the Ring. "He'll eat us all, if He gets it, eat all the world." This is consistent with the possessiveness of evil; Sauron devours everything, making it no longer something free and independent, but a part of himself.

Originally Gollum was only going to guide Sam and Frodo to the edge of Mordor and then be set free. But now he offers to take the hobbits into Mordor, through a secret passage he discovered when he escaped from Sauron. Frodo decides to trust him once again.

Gollum leads the hobbits into Ithilien, which lies along the mountains that form the western border of Mordor. Ithilien is a beautiful land, full of forests and streams. Not too long ago it was part of

Gondor, which lies just across the river. But now Ithilien is held by Sauron's forces, and their presence is revealed by felled trees, pits of stinking refuse, and the eye of Sauron carved into stones and trees.

NOTE: Frodo as a Saint   Frodo's quest can be interpreted as spiritual. While he journeys toward Mordor, the stronghold of evil, he must struggle with the evil within himself, as symbolized by the Ring and the temptation to use it. By taking on the quest to destroy the Ring, Frodo is sacrificing his own desires to save the rest of the world. And through his sufferings, he's transformed. Sam notices this change in Frodo. While Frodo is sleeping, Sam sees a light shining within him. Frodo's face looks peaceful, very ancient, but also beautiful. This serenity and inner light is often used to characterize saints.

The hobbits find themselves in the midst of a battle between some men of Gondor and an army of Southrons, men from the south who have come to join forces with the evil Sauron. Tolkien takes this opportunity to make a point about the tragedy of war. One of the Southrons falls dead near Sam. In a sudden moment of insight, Sam wonders about the man's name and whether he fought only because he had been deceived or threatened by his leaders. Maybe, Sam reflects, he would have preferred to stay home and live in peace. Is Tolkien hinting that the *common men* in the enemy's armies really aren't all that different from those who fight on the side of good?

When the battle ends, the hobbits meet Faramir, who is captain of the Gondor army and also Boromir's brother. Compare this meeting with the one between Aragorn, Legolas, and Gimli, and Éomer, captain of a group of Riders of Rohan. Éomer was under orders to detain all strangers; Faramir is ordered to kill them. But like Éomer, Faramir tempers orders with his own judgment. Neither of them is likely to give the excuse that he was only following orders if he should ever do something wrong, just as so many Nazis pleaded after World War II. Here, Tolkien introduces another aspect of free will: you must be willing to accept responsibility for your own actions and not blindly follow another's orders if you think they're wrong.

Faramir also serves as a contrast to his brother. Unlike Boromir, Faramir does not love war; his only purpose in fighting is to protect the home he loves. Also, unlike the proud Boromir, Faramir is not tempted to take the Ring. He's wise enough to know that Sauron's evil power can't be used to bring about good.

BOOK IV, CHAPTERS 6–10

With misgivings, Faramir allows the hobbits to continue their quest. Gollum guides Frodo and Sam into Mordor, betraying them there.

*

Gollum is captured by the men of Gondor and would have been killed, except for Frodo's intervention. Frodo at this point has come a long way from Bag End. He now accepts responsibility for others, taking Gollum under his protection to save his life. He also speaks with Faramir as with an equal, showing his rise in status. Tolkien even compares Frodo to Aragorn: When Gollum balks at being blindfolded, Frodo says that all three of them will be blindfolded, just as Aragorn insisted in Lórien when Gimli the dwarf was unfairly singled out for similar treatment.

Against Faramir's advice, the hobbits follow Gollum past Minas Morgul, once a stronghold of good, but now held by Sauron. From there they climb a long series of stairs that leads to a secret passage over the mountains and into Mordor.

An important incident occurs before they enter the secret tunnel. Gollum returns from his wanderings to find Frodo and Sam sleeping peacefully. He is debating with himself, and Sméagol, his good side, seems to be winning. He gives Frodo a touch that is almost a caress; for a moment, he himself looks like an old weary hobbit—"starved, pitiable." But when Sam awakens and accuses him of sneaking, the moment is past and Gollum reverts to his evil self. Here you see why some people consider Gollum such a tragic character: when it seems possible he might be reformed by the goodness of others, a moment of misunderstanding ruins everything.

Gollum now leads the hobbits into a trap. The tunnel they must take is the lair of Shelob, a monstrous spiderlike creature, the mother of the spiders that attacked Bilbo and the dwarves in *The Hobbit*. As Shelob advances on her prey, Sam has a sudden vision of Galadriel and the phial of starlight she gave Frodo. Frodo holds out the phial, and as his hope increases so does the light, until it seems to be a brilliant flame in his hand. Frodo calls out some elvish words, but it's as if another voice is speaking through him. Some readers interpret these things—Sam's vision, the light of the phial, and Frodo's words of power—as the emergence of some inner resource that the hobbits had previously been unaware of. Others see it as a sign that Sam and Frodo are not alone, but are being aided by some power that works through them. Before the blaze of the phial and the threat of Frodo's sword, Shelob backs away, and the hobbits flee out the other end of the tunnel, into Mordor.

NOTE: Shelob, the Personification of Greed
When Gollum said that Sauron would eat the whole world, he was speaking figuratively. Shelob, on the other hand, desires literally to eat all living things. She personifies greed, showing in a horrifying way its destructiveness. Sauron's ambition is to make all other wills into an extension of his own. Shelob's ambition is to destroy not only will, but life, so that in all the world she's the only creature left alive.

Sam and Frodo haven't escaped Shelob yet. She emerges from her tunnel and attacks Frodo. With great courage and the help of Galadriel's phial, Sam manages to drive Shelob back into her tunnel. But when he returns to his master, he finds Frodo lying pale and lifeless from Shelob's sting. Believing that Frodo is dead, Sam takes the Ring and leaves, intending to carry on the quest—the destruction of the Ring—himself. The Ring is a physical burden, bowing Sam's head down to the ground. Remember that Tolkien often manipulates the physical characteristics of things to signify something different about them—for example, Gollum's momentary change into an old, tired hobbit to signify that his gentler personality, Sméagol, was in control. What do you think is the significance of the weight of the Ring and Sam's ability to bear it?

Just then, Sam hears the voices of orcs and follows them. The orcs discover Frodo's body and carry it back to their tower. Sam realizes that his love for Frodo is greater than any sense of duty, and he runs after the orcs to die defending his master. How would you characterize Sam's act? Is it noble or foolish? How do his actions relate to Tolkien's theme of the importance of friendship?

As Sam follows the orcs, he overhears their two leaders talking and learns that Frodo isn't dead, but only paralyzed. He calls himself a fool; he knew in his heart that Frodo was alive, but didn't listen. Brandishing Sting, he chases after the orcs. But the great gates of the fortress clang shut behind the orcs, locking Sam out.

PART THREE: THE RETURN OF THE KING

BOOK V, CHAPTERS 1–5

Sauron's army begins its siege of Minas Tirith, the capital of Gondor.

*

Gandalf and Pippin arrive in Minas Tirith amid preparations for war. They meet with Denethor,

Boromir's father, the steward of Gondor. Pippin offers his allegiance to Denethor, and the steward accepts. What moves Pippin to do this?

NOTE: Minas Tirith is the capital of Gondor, one of the ancient kingdoms of the Númenóreans, a noble and long-lived race of men. The last king of Gondor disappeared in a previous encounter with evil, and since then a series of stewards have ruled, safeguarding the throne until a king should appear. This is the throne that Aragorn is heir to.

Just as some readers compare the men of Rohan to the Anglo-Saxons, they compare Gondor to such ancient kingdoms as Rome or Greece. Like a Roman city, Minas Tirith is immense and beautiful. The hall of the king is imposing, and the steward is a subtle and learned man, wise in the ways of politics. Next to him, King Théoden seems like just a kindly old man. But there is also a sense of barrenness here: the dead tree in the courtyard, the cold granite of the great hall, and the steward himself, who shows no trace of human warmth. Compare this to the description of Théoden's hall, Meduseld, with its hanging tapestries and many-colored, richly carved pillars. Look for further contrast between Gondor and Rohan, and try to determine what Tolkien is saying about the two cultures.

The story now returns to the point when Gandalf and Pippin left the others, a day's journey out of Isengard. Aragorn, Merry, Legolas, and Gimli remain with the king and his company. As they make ready to depart, a company of riders appear. They are Rangers from the north, like Aragorn, and have come to help him. That night, Merry swears fealty to King Théoden. How does this differ from the scene where Pippin swears fealty to Denethor?

Aragorn now takes a fateful step, for the first time going against Gandalf's advice. At the end of Book III, Gandalf had warned him against using the *palantír*, saying that it was not yet time to reveal themselves to Sauron. Aragorn now judges for himself that the time has come and that he has the strength to face Sauron. He wrests the stone from Sauron and reveals himself as the heir to Gondor's throne. This strikes fear into Sauron's heart. Aragorn hopes also that it will move Sauron to a hasty attack, which will be ill-timed and unprepared. The *palantír* shows Aragorn an unforeseen danger approaching Gondor from the south, which only Aragorn can act to avert. With new resolve, Aragorn decides to take the Paths of the Dead, caverns that lead right through the mountains, and that are haunted by spirits of the dead.

This is an important point in Aragorn's life. He steps out from under Gandalf's wing, making two crucial decisions without consulting others: he uses the *palantír*, and he accepts his destiny that he must travel the Paths of the Dead. Both are supreme tests of his power. He has passed one, and it remains to be seen if he'll pass the other. If he fails, he stands to lose everything, including the throne of Gondor and his love, Arwen.

The way to the Paths of the Dead passes through Dunharrow, a place of safety where Théoden's people, led by Éowyn, have taken refuge. When

Éowyn learns of Aragorn's plan, she is fearful and tries to talk him out of it. When she sees he won't be swayed, she asks to go with him, but Aragorn refuses.

If you read their conversation closely, you will see that there is a lot being said between the lines. When Aragorn tells Éowyn that his heart dwells in Rivendell, he's referring to his love for Arwen. Do you think Éowyn understands that he loves another? When she says that the Rangers follow him through the Paths of the Dead only because they love him and won't be parted from him, she's declaring her love for Aragorn—she doesn't want to be parted from him either.

Notice the formal speech used here. Éowyn calls Aragorn "thee" and Aragorn calls her "lady." The formal words underscore the fact that they are speaking with great restraint. By its sharp contrast with what the two are feeling, the formal speech also heightens the sense of suppressed emotion boiling beneath the surface.

NOTE: As mentioned earlier, some readers criticize Tolkien for ignoring women in his work, or for only idealizing them in such beautiful but unreachable characters as Arwen and Galadriel. But in Éowyn, Tolkien presents a woman who is all too human, someone whom female readers of his book can identify with. She suffers from unrequited love for Aragorn. She also suffers from the restricted role women have to play. Éowyn says she fears nothing but being caged: "To stay behind bars, until use and old age accept them, and all chance of doing great deeds is gone beyond recall or desire." Through his sympathetic portrayal of Éowyn, Tolkien here expresses his awareness of the needs and desires of women, even though he may neglect them through most of the book.

Legolas and Gimli travel with Aragorn and the Rangers through the Paths of the Dead. This area is haunted by the spirits of men who had broken their oath to fight against Sauron in the last war. Aragorn calls on the dead to fulfill their oath now and win peace for themselves. In his ability to command the dead, Aragorn proves his power and his claim to the throne, for only Isildur's heir could hold the dead to their oath. Ironically, here he becomes a king of sorts: the townspeople flee before him and his company, calling him the King of the Dead.

King Théoden arrives in Dunharrow soon after Aragorn's departure. He immediately prepares to ride with his army to Minas Tirith, to help defend that city against Sauron. Merry is dejected to learn he'll be left behind. But a young Rider named Dernhelm helps the hobbit. Earlier in the day Merry had noticed the warrior looking at him. The hobbit had seen in Dernhelm's face the hopelessness of someone who yearns solely for death. Now Dernhelm whispers in his ear, "Where will wants not, a way opens"—a rephrasing of the old proverb "Where there's a will, there's a way." Merry rides to war hidden under Dernhelm's cloak. Remember Dernhelm's words and desire for death, because they will have greater significance later.

Meanwhile, in Minas Tirith, Faramir has arrived from Ithilien and tells his father, Denethor, of the meeting with Frodo. For the first time Denethor learns of the quest to destroy the Ring. He thinks the quest is doomed to failure and is angry with Faramir for not bringing him the Ring. His other son, Boromir, he says, would have done so. With angry words, Denethor sends his son to the battlefront, wishing Faramir had died instead of Boromir.

Later, when Faramir is seriously wounded by the captain of the ringwraiths, Denethor remorsefully realizes that he also loves Faramir. The old man falls into despair; with Faramir's death the line of stewards will end. Believing that Sauron will triumph, Denethor sees no reason to go on fighting. He resolves to commit suicide by burning Faramir and himself on a funeral pyre.

BOOK V, CHAPTERS 6–10

The arrival of the Riders of Rohan turns the tide of battle. After Minas Tirith is saved, Aragorn leads the armies to the very gates of Mordor, where they are surrounded by Sauron's forces.

*

At that moment, when all seems lost, the men of Rohan arrive and join the battle. The captain of the ringwraiths, mounted on his winged steed, flies over the battlefield, striking despair into the hearts of men. But unlike Denethor, Théoden refuses to succumb to despair. He calls to his men, "Fear no darkness!" Perhaps having already overcome the despair induced by Gríma the Wormtongue, Théoden is now immune to it.

Théoden's horse is struck by a dart from the captain of the ringwraiths and falls on its master. As the wraith swoops down for the kill, he is challenged by Dernhelm, now revealed as Éowyn. With Merry's help, she kills the ringwraith. In this way another prophecy is fulfilled, that the ringwraith would not die at the hand of any man.

Merry's sword proves to carry unthought-of significance. It was made long ago to be used against the Witch-lord of Angmar, the leader of the ringwraiths. The man who made the sword went to defeat and death. But his efforts were not entirely fruitless, because Merry found the sword in the barrow and carried it all the way to Minas Tirith. Only this sword could have harmed the ringwraith. Through details such as this, Tolkien shows the workings of a greater purpose, one that men cannot follow, because it works too slowly, taking unknown years to bear fruit. Tolkien's message seems to be that even though something you have done may appear futile at the time, in years to come it may prove to be of great importance.

While Éowyn faces the ringwraith, Gandalf is inside the city, saving Faramir from his father's madness. But Denethor, in his pride and despair, cannot be stopped from killing himself. Denethor gives several reasons for wanting to die. He believes that Sauron will win the war. But he also knows that Aragorn is coming to claim his throne, and Denethor will have to relinquish his power. Since he cannot have things as he wants them, the steward would rather die than serve another. Compare Denethor's death with Théoden's. One gives in to despair, the other dies resisting it.

Like Saruman, Denethor had a *palantír*, which he used to watch the growing strength of Sauron. Denethor believed that he controlled the *palantír*, but Sauron actually controlled it and presented a distorted picture to the steward, one intended to induce despair.

NOTE: Despair as the Weapon of Evil   When Denethor falls into despair, he brings about the deaths of others as well as himself. If not for Denethor, Gandalf would have been in the battlefield and possibly could have prevented Théoden's death and the wounding of Éowyn and Merry. Gandalf says that this is the working of Sauron. The ringwraiths also use despair as a weapon. Few men can resist the power of their cries, which make men cower in despair and stop fighting. Despair, then, causes people to abandon their roles in the grand design, and to fail to do their allotted tasks. In this way evil prevails.

For now, the battle is over, but Faramir, Éowyn, and Merry all lie in the Houses of Healing. Seemingly nothing can cure them, until Aragorn arrives and calls them back from their dreaming. There is a saying in Gondor that the hands of a king are the hands of the healer, and now it is whispered that a king has come. But Aragorn slips away without claiming his throne. Remember when Aragorn refused to leave his sword outside King Théoden's hall? You can see now how he has changed. Then he placed his pride above peace, until Gandalf rebuked him. Now, he humbles himself rather than stir up controversy by his claim to kingship. For the moment it's more important to have a united front against Mordor.

Meanwhile, Gandalf counsels the armies to march

to Mordor itself, not with hope of victory, but only to draw Sauron's attention, so that Frodo, the Ring-bearer, may pass through the enemy lands unnoticed. If Frodo fails, they shall all die or be enslaved. Even if Frodo succeeds, they may still die. The importance of Frodo's task also places the heroic deeds of the warriors in true perspective. For all their courage and losses, their battles have been only a distraction. The real battle lies with the two hobbits, Frodo and Sam, who struggle alone through Mordor. With them alone lies victory or defeat. It's the moral battle, not the physical one, that determines the fate of the world.

Aragorn again shows his wisdom as a leader. As the armies approach Mordor, there are many who cannot face the horror of that land. Instead of calling them cowards, Aragorn gives them an opportunity to fight with honor, sending them instead to retake the fortress of Cair Andros. Although difficult, this is a task they can face, even if they should die, and so he saves them from giving in to despair.

At the Black Gate of Mordor the heralds call on Sauron to surrender. In answer, an envoy called the Mouth of Sauron emerges from the gates. In this character you can see Tolkien's theme that evil destroys free will and identity. The Mouth of Sauron has forgotten his name and now exists only to serve his master's will. He holds out Sam's sword, an elven cloak, and Frodo's coat of mail. He offers a bargain: Frodo will be released if they swear peace with Sauron. Gandalf rejects those terms. Why? And why should Sauron even bother to bargain when the odds are overwhelmingly in his favor? Why is it important to him that they submit?

Seemingly, all hope is gone. As the Black Gate

swings open, Sauron's mighty army descends on the small force. The arrival of the eagles as Book V ends may be a sign of hope, but will they alone be able to turn the tide of battle?

BOOK VI, CHAPTERS 1–5

The story returns to Sam and Frodo, who at last succeed in destroying the Ring. Sauron is defeated, and amidst great rejoicing, Aragorn is crowned king of Gondor.

*

As Sam stands outside the tower of Cirith Ungol, wondering how he will rescue Frodo, he is tempted by power of the Ring. But his love for Frodo and his simple hobbit-sense save him. He has no desire to rule the world, but wants only to tend his own patch of land. Sam passes the test, and like Galadriel, he diminishes from the powerful figure that the Ring makes him seem, and becomes only himself, a small frightened hobbit.

Sam hears the sounds of fighting in the tower. This fighting reveals the weakness of evil; the orcs cannot cooperate and are killing each other in petty arguments. Finally, only two orcs are left alive. Driving them off, Sam rescues Frodo, and the two have a tender reunion. But a terrible change comes over Frodo when Sam hands him back the Ring. Grabbing the Ring, Frodo calls Sam a thief. Before his eyes, Sam seems to have suddenly turned into a greedy orc. But the negative effect on Frodo of the Ring's evil power quickly passes.

Dressed in orc uniforms, Sam and Frodo leave

the fortress to begin the last stage of their journey. The land of Mordor is a dark, desolate place, with no living things but some twisted brambles. Even here, however, a star is visible in the sky. The symbolism of star and shadow is carried to its logical conclusion. A shadow may obscure the stars for a while, but the stars will always be shining far above, out of the reach of darkness. Is Tolkien saying that good can never be overcome by evil, but will always triumph in the end?

Caught between the pull of the Ring and the pressure of Sauron's will, Frodo is so weary he can hardly walk. He and Sam discard everything they don't need. Symbolically, they seem to be stripping themselves to the core of their humanity: the indomitable will to carry on to the end. Sam is the leader at this point. He cares for Frodo, leading him onward and even carrying him when Frodo's strength fails. It is Sam's memory of the Shire that gives him the will to go on in the face of the horror of Mordor.

As they creep up the slopes of Mount Doom, they are attacked by Gollum. Sam deals with Gollum while Frodo struggles on alone. Sam is tempted to kill the miserable creature, but spares him, as Bilbo and Frodo did before him. Having borne the Ring even a little while, he understands and pities Gollum's agony.

Sam follows after Frodo and finds him standing before the Crack of Doom. There, Frodo's will fails, and he claims the Ring for himself. But Gollum struggles with him, biting off the finger with the Ring and, still gloating, accidentally falls into the fiery abyss. With the destruction of the Ring, Sauron is vanquished forever: his armies are scattered or destroyed, and his towers crumble. Sam and Frodo are rescued from the destruction by the eagles, and the two hobbits are welcomed with great praise by the victorious army. This is the climax of the book, where the two halves of the story, the war and the quest, meet in victory. The rest of the book serves as a gradual winding down from this climax, as Tolkien ties up loose ends.

The destruction of Sauron coincides with the beginning of spring, which has long symbolized spiritual renewal. Tolkien makes many references to renewal and to the end of barrenness. Frodo himself, now free of the Ring, seems to have recovered his old sense of gaiety. An eagle announces Sauron's fall to the people of Minas Tirith with a song that sounds almost like a Christian psalm referring to the resurrection of Christ. Éowyn experiences a rebirth of sorts, when she falls in love with Faramir. She no longer desires death or glory in battle. Instead she wants to be a healer "and love all things that grow and are not barren." As a final symbol of the end of barrenness, Aragorn finds a sapling to replace the white tree of Gondor that had stood withered in the courtyard for so long.

This is a time of triumph for Aragorn. He is crowned king of Gondor and marries Arwen, Elrond's daughter. But there is an element of tragedy mixed in with his joy. To marry him, Arwen has had to give up immortality. She is now doomed to die and so is forever separated from her father and her brothers, who will pass over to the Blessed Realm and live there. Besides this personal loss, Aragorn also feels the loss of many beautiful things, such as Lórien, which will pass with the destruction of the Ring. This mixture of tragedy with joy is characteristic of Tolkien.

BOOK VI, CHAPTERS 6–9

The hobbits return to the Shire, where they find that evil has been at work in their absence. The Shire is saved, but Frodo never recovers from his many wounds.

*

The four hobbits, accompanied by Gandalf, now depart for home. After stopping in Rivendell to visit Bilbo, they arrive in Bree, where there has been trouble with ruffians from the south. The travelers learn that things are not well in the Shire either. Gandalf seems to know more about the trouble than he lets on. The hobbits assume he will set things right, but Gandalf tells them he isn't going to the Shire. His time of helping out is over, and they're quite capable of doing it themselves. In fact, he tells them, this is what they were trained for. What do you think he means by that remark?

The hobbits continue on to the Shire and find that Saruman and his men have taken over and are tearing down buildings and cutting trees. Now you can see most clearly how their journeys have changed the four friends. They are not intimidated, but set out with determination to rouse the inhabitants of the Shire to throw out Saruman's ruffians. Frodo, however, refuses to fight. He has learned that no one has the right to take the life of another, no matter how just that death may seem. He extends his sympathy to all—the good, the evil, and the misguided—because he knows that no one started out evil and that those who do fall into evil suffer the most of all. Saruman himself appears as a pitiable figure, and even his attempt to kill Frodo doesn't change Frodo's resolve to let him go free.

Gríma the Wormtongue is still with Saruman. Like Gollum, he has been deformed by evil and now crawls after Saruman like a dog. Frodo offers him a chance to turn away from Saruman. Gríma seems to feel a touch of hope, but Saruman destroys it by telling the others about Gríma's evil deeds. Gríma turns on his master and kills him, only to be killed himself by the overzealous hobbits.

Sam uses Galadriel's gift, a box of soil from Lórien, to restore the beauty of the Shire. He finds that he's become a hero like Merry and Pippin. Ironically enough, Frodo's deeds are overlooked. The folks of the Shire are more concerned with the events in their own small country than with far-off happenings in places they've never seen. They don't seem to understand the danger that would have faced them if Frodo's quest had failed.

Frodo has not emerged from his trials unscathed, either physically or spiritually. The memory and the effect of the Ring stay with him. "It is gone forever," he says, "and now all is dark and empty." Like Gollum, he feels lost and empty without the Ring. Although Frodo has won peace for the land, he himself cannot enjoy it. He travels with Bilbo, Gandalf, Elrond, and Galadriel over the sea to the serenely beautiful Blessed Realm, leaving Sam to return home to his wife and child in the Shire.

Some readers see this as a happy ending. Others

feel sad that Frodo's selfless quest has ended un-
happily for him. Which view do you agree with?
Is this a pessimistic or an optimistic ending? Why
do you feel that way?

A STEP BEYOND

Test and Answers

TEST

1. The Lord of the Rings is   _____
   A. Frodo   B. Gandalf   C. Sauron

2. *The Hobbit*   _____
   A. was originally published as a children's book
   B. is Tolkien's most important book
   C. is about the corrupting effect of power

3. Smaug the dragon is a symbol of   _____
   A. the destructive forces of nature
   B. greed
   C. the evils of technology

4. Which of the following are considered   _____ by some readers to be references to Christianity in *The Lord of the Rings*?
   I. *Lembas*
   II. Gandalf's staff
   III. The Blessed Realm
   A. I, II, and III   B. II and III only
   C. I and III only

5. Gollum represents the   _____
   A. potential for evil that Frodo must struggle against within himself
   B. dangers of showing mercy to evildoers

   C. power of the Ring to corrupt even
      those with the best intentions

6. The Ring represents the   _____
   A. dangers of nuclear weapons
   B. corrupting effect of absolute power
   C. power of the council of wizards

7. Tom Bombadil and Treebeard   _____
   A. add humor to *The Lord of the Rings*
   B. are representatives of the natural
      world
   C. are unwitting victims of evil

8. Tolkien's only well-developed female   _____
   character is
   A. Éowyn   B. Galadriel   C. Arwen

9. The hobbits   _____
   I. are Tolkien's invention
   II. represent the potential for greatness
      in ordinary people
   III. represent disadvantaged minorities in
       today's society
   A. I and III only   B. II only
   C. I and II only

10. Tolkien would most likely agree with which   _____
    of these statements about war?
    A. War is sometimes necessary to combat
       evil.
    B. War offers an opportunity for man to
       display his heroism.
    C. Wars should never be fought, for any
       reason.

11. Would Tolkien agree with the phrase "Power corrupts, absolute power corrupts absolutely"? Give evidence to support your answer.

12. Discuss how Tolkien uses the imagery of stars and shadow as symbols for good and evil.

13. Discuss two ways that Tolkien draws your attention to language in *The Lord of the Rings* and *The Hobbit*.

ANSWERS

1. C   **2.** A   **3.** B   **4.** C   **5.** A   **6.** B
7. B   **8.** A   **9.** C   **10.** A

11. You could take either side of this question. If you say yes, discuss the corrupting influence of the Ring, using specific examples. Point to the fact that anybody, even Gandalf, will fall into the temptation to use it, and that once he uses it, he will become evil, like Sauron.

You could argue from the opposite view, as well. Point to the fact that Frodo, Bilbo, Faramir, and others were able to resist the Ring. Those who fall prey to the Ring's power possess some character flaw, such as Boromir's pride and desire to rule others. Also point to the fact that there are different kinds of power. The elves possess the power to heal and the power to understand. It is only the power to dominate others that seems to corrupt.

12. To answer this question, you must first show how Tolkien creates an association between stars and good, and between shadow and evil. For instance, Gandalf refers to Sauron as "the Shadow." Tolkien's elves, on the other hand, are closely associated with stars. You will find specific examples in the story section of this guide.

Next, you must show how the images of star and shadow serve as symbols for good and evil. For example, just as shadows can hide the stars, evil can hide all traces of good, leading some people to despair and believe that there is no good. But like the stars, good cannot be obliterated by evil and will endure no matter how desperate things seem.

13. You have a variety of options here. You can illustrate the way Tolkien gives his characters different styles of speech. For example, you may want to discuss the speech of the trolls, the goblins, and Gollum in *The Hobbit*. You can also mention that sometimes language seems to have a power of its own. For example, Tom Bombadil uses language to give him power over things, and the language of Mordor brings a shadow over Rivendell when Gandalf speaks it there. Finally, Tolkien's use of invented languages draws attention to the variety of languages in the world and to the fact that his languages seem suited to the people who use them. You may want to point out the harshness of the language of Mordor and the grandeur of the language of the elves. Other ways that Tolkien draws your attention to language have been discussed throughout this guide.

Term Paper Ideas and other Topics for Writing

The Novels

1. Explore the elements of the old traditions of mythology, legends, and folklore that Tolkien drew on. Then discuss his changes to make these traditions acceptable to a modern audience.

2. Around the time that Tolkien was writing *The Lord of the Rings*, he also wrote a lecture, "On Fairy-stories," which can be found under "Tree and Leaf" in *The Tolkien Reader* (New York: Ballantine Books, 1966). Discuss the ideas he presents in that lecture, and show how he applied them to *The Lord of the Rings*.

3. Discuss the ways in which *The Hobbit* seems designed for children. Compare *The Hobbit* to a children's classic, such as *The Wind in the Willows*, or to another book supposedly written for children but also enjoyed by adults, such as *Alice in Wonderland*.

4. Although Tolkien isn't the first writer of fantasy novels, he is often considered the "father of fantasy." Review the history of the fantasy novel, and examine Tolkien's contributions to the genre.

5. Discuss similarities between *The Hobbit* and *The Lord of the Rings*. In what ways may *The Lord of the Rings* be said to be an expanded version of *The Hobbit*? In what ways is it more than just an elaborated version of *The Hobbit*'s plot?

The Author

1. Discuss elements of Christianity that appear in the trilogy. Also discuss the belief of some readers that *The Lord of the Rings* is a Christian allegory. Tell whether or not you agree, and why.

2. While he was writing his books, Tolkien read them aloud to a group of friends called the Inklings. Two other authors of fantasy also belonged to the Inklings, C. S. Lewis and Charles Williams. Pick a fantasy novel by one of these authors and compare it with Tolkien's work.

How are they similar, and how are they different? Point out where you think the authors may have influenced each others' works.

3. In what ways did Tolkien's life influence his books?

Characters

1. Compare the characters of Frodo and Bilbo. Then discuss the significance of the differences between the two characters.

2. The different races in *The Hobbit* and *The Lord of the Rings* each have their own "personalities." Choose three of these races, and briefly describe their characteristics. Be sure to include at least one strength and one weakness for each race. Then compare and contrast the three races.

3. Choose two of Tolkien's evil characters and show how they fit into his concept of evil. Next, discuss how Tolkien's ideas about evil can be applied to events in the world today.

4. Compare and contrast the characters of Frodo and Aragorn as they develop through the course of *The Lord of the Rings.*

5. It has been commented that Tolkien's books are written in such a way as to invite comparisons between characters. Choose two characters and show how Tolkien draws comparisons between them. Discuss the implications of these comparisons.

Themes

1. How does Tolkien develop his theme of the nature of heroism? Give examples.

2. Discuss elements of elitism in Tolkien's books. Explain why some people criticize this elitism, while others defend it. Be sure to include examples of what some readers see as Tolkien's male, upper-class prejudices.

3. The Shire, Rivendell, and Lórien all represent various aspects of Tolkien's ideal society. Compare and contrast these different societies. Which would you prefer to live in? Why?

4. Discuss Tolkien's concept of the relationship between free will and destiny. Relate it to philosophical and theological debates about this question. Do you think man has free will?

5. Examine the relationship among loyalty to an individual, loyalty to a small group, and loyalty to all of mankind in Tolkien's books. Especially examine instances where loyalties conflict. How do the characters resolve their dilemmas? What implications can you draw about Tolkien's beliefs from these instances?

6. Make a list of the qualities associated with the forces of good in *The Lord of the Rings* and those associated with the forces of evil. Discuss any interesting patterns that emerge. For instance, do good and evil form a mirror image of each other? How do these qualities relate to Tolkien's themes?

7. Discuss the relationship between man and nature expressed in Tolkien's books. Mention characters that Tolkien uses to represent nature.

8. Look at how Tolkien developed the Everyman theme in his books. Compare Tolkien's hobbits with the characters who appear to function as Everyman in other novels.

Further Reading
CRITICAL WORKS

Carpenter, Humphrey. *The Inklings.* Boston: Houghton Mifflin, 1979.

———. *Tolkien: A Biography.* Boston: Houghton Mifflin, 1977. An authorized biography; contains valuable insights.

Carpenter, Humphrey, and Christopher Tolkien, eds. *The Letters of J. R. R. Tolkien.* Boston: Houghton Mifflin, 1981.

Carter, Lin. *Tolkien: A Look Behind "The Lord of the Rings."* New York: Ballantine, 1969. Discusses ancient legends and epics that seem to have influenced Tolkien; also discusses the development of the fantasy genre.

Crabbe, Katharyn F. *J. R. R. Tolkien.* New York: Ungar, 1981. Easy reading.

Foster, Robert. *A Guide to Middle Earth.* New York: Ballantine, 1975. Handy guide to the people and places of Middle-earth.

Grotta-Kurska, Daniel. *J. R. R. Tolkien: Architect of Middle Earth.* New York: Warner, 1976. Biography.

Helms, Randel. *Tolkien's World.* Boston: Houghton Mifflin, 1974.

Hillegas, Mark R., ed. *Shadows of the Imagination: The Fantasies of C. S. Lewis, J. R. R. Tolkien, and Charles Williams.* Carbondale: Southern Illinois University Press, 1969.

Isaacs, Neil D., and Rose A. Zimbardo, eds. *Tolkien and the Critics: Essays on J. R. R. Tolkien's "The Lord of the Rings."* Notre Dame: University of Notre Dame Press, 1968.

———. *Tolkien: New Critical Perspectives.* Lexington: University Press of Kentucky, 1981. Collection of essays.

"Frodo and Aragorn: The Concept of Hero" and "Tolkien and the Rhetoric of Childhood" are exceptionally good.

Kocher, Paul H. *Master of Middle Earth: The Fiction of J. R. R. Tolkien.* Boston: Houghton Mifflin, 1972. Critical discussion of Tolkien's works, including his lesser-known poetry and stories.

Noel, Ruth S. *The Mythology of Middle-earth.* Boston: Houghton Mifflin, 1977. Compares elements of Tolkien's novels with various legends and myths.

Ready, William. *The Tolkien Relation.* New York: Warner, 1968. Interesting insights.

Shippey, T. A. *The Road to Middle Earth.* Boston: Houghton Mifflin, 1983. Thoughtful discussion of Tolkien's fiction by a fellow philologist.

Urang, Gunnar. *Shadows of Heaven: Religion and Fantasy in the Writings of C. S. Lewis, Charles Williams, and J. R. R. Tolkien.* New York: Pilgrim, 1971.

West, Richard C. *Tolkien Criticism: An Annotated Checklist.* Rev. ed. Kent, Ohio: Kent State University Press, 1981.

AUTHOR'S SELECTED
OTHER WORKS

Tolkien wrote very little fiction besides *The Hobbit* and *The Lord of the Rings.* This list contains his better-known stories and poetry, as well as relevant nonfiction. You'll find a complete listing of all his fiction and nonfiction in the back of Humphrey Carpenter's *Tolkien: A Biography.*

Fiction

1947	"Leaf by Niggle"
1949	"Farmer Giles of Ham"
1967	"Smith of Wooten Major"
1977	*The Silmarillion*

Poetry

1962   "The Adventures of Tom Bombadil"

Nonfiction

1936   "*Beowulf:* The Monsters and the Critics"
        (essay)
1947   "On Fairy-stories" (essay)
1953   "The Homecoming of Beorhtnoth
        Beorhthelm's Son" (essay)
1975   *Sir Gawain and the Green Knight, Pearl, and Sir
        Orfeo* (a translation of three medieval poems)

Chronology of Middle-earth

This chronology of Middle-earth is taken from the more complete chronology in the appendices in *The Return of the King* and from information in *The Silmarillion*.

First Age

Eru, the One, creates the world with the help of the Valar, his servants, who dwell in the Blessed Realm. The elves, dwarves, and ents are created. Morgoth, one of the Valar who has turned evil, breeds a race of orcs.

Many of the elves are brought by the Valar to the Blessed Realm. Morgoth steals three beautiful gems, the Silmarils, from the elves and carries them back to Middle-earth. A host of elves follow him to recover the jewels.

At this time, men are created. The Dúnedain, a noble race of men, join the fight against Morgoth. Eärendil, who is half man, half elf, sails to the forbidden Blessed Realm. He asks help of the Valar, who defeat Morgoth.

Second Age

0–40   The Dúnedain are given the island of Númenor to settle.

1000   Sauron, Morgoth's servant, builds a stronghold in Mordor.

1500   Elves, deceived by Sauron, forge the Rings of Power.

1600   Sauron forges the One Ring.

1693–1700   War erupts between the elves and Sauron. In 1697, Elrond, a son of Eärendil, founds Rivendell. In 1700, Sauron is defeated.

3262   Númenóreans capture Sauron, who has risen again.

3262–3319   Sauron succeeds in corrupting the Númenóreans, who rebel against the Valar in 3319. Númenor is destroyed.

3320   Elendil, who has led a few faithful Numenoreans to Middle-earth, founds Arnor in the north and Gondor in the south.

3429–3441   Elves and men form an alliance against Sauron, who has reappeared. He is defeated in 3441. Elendil's son Isildur takes Sauron's Ring.

Third Age

2   Isildur is slain by orcs; Sauron's Ring is lost.

1050   Hobbits first appear. Around this time, wizards also appear.

1409–1974   Arnor falls in a war against the ringwraiths. The Dúnedain of the North eventually become Rangers.

1975   Ringwraiths are defeated in the North.

1981   Dwarves flee Moria after a Balrog appears.

1999   Dwarf kingdom under the Lonely Mountain is founded.

2000   Ringwraiths begin war against Gondor.

2050   Rule of stewards in Gondor begins.

2460   Sauron (the Necromancer) appears in Dol Guldor in Mirkwood.

2463   White Council is formed. Gollum finds the Ring. Orcs multiply in the Misty Mountains.

2770   Smaug descends on the dwarf kingdom in the Lonely Mountain.

2890   Bilbo is born.

2931   Aragorn is born.

2941   Bilbo sets out on his adventure with the dwarves and finds Sauron's Ring. The orcs are defeated in the Battle of the Five Armies. Sauron is driven out of Dol Guldor by the White Council.

2942   Bilbo returns to the Shire. Sauron returns to Mordor.

2951   Aragorn and Arwen first meet.

2957–2980   Aragorn, incognito, joins first the Riders of Rohan, then the men of Gondor, in their fight against Sauron's forces.

2968   Frodo is born.

3001   Bilbo holds a farewell birthday party.

The Great Years

3018   September: Frodo leaves Bag End, pursued by Black Riders.

October: Frodo arrives in Rivendell.

3019   January: Gandalf dies in battle with the Balrog.

February: Merry and Pippin are captured by orcs. Aragorn, Legolas, and Gimli follow in an attempt to rescue them. Frodo and Sam begin their long trek to Mordor.

March 5: Gandalf breaks Saruman's staff.

March 13: Frodo is captured by orcs just inside Mordor.

3019 March 25: The Ring is destroyed.

May 1: Aragorn is crowned king of Gondor.

November: Hobbits return to the Shire.

3021 September: Frodo passes over the sea to the Blessed Realm.

The Critics

Thoughts on Frodo

Today's reader of modern narrative, however medieval its spirit, may be reluctant to accept a truly medieval monster—a dragon or fiend—but he is accustomed to accepting internal conflict. Frodo the monster-queller might not be credible. But Frodo tortured by growing evil in his own nature . . . is believable and compelling. . . . In the final moment, standing at the Cracks of Doom, Frodo succumbs to the darkness within him. He puts the Ring on his finger, claimed by it even as he claims it. . . . For man always loses to the monster at last. Frodo is defeated as surely as Beowulf is. . . .

Although Frodo recovers from the battle, he can no longer be what he was. . . . The fairy-tale hero, inconspicuous and unassuming, has been made to suffer the bitterness and loss of the medieval epic hero. Like Beowulf, like Arthur, he loses the last battle and pays a heavy price for his struggle. Such an ending is dreadfully inappropriate. . . .

And that, of course, is just Tolkien's point. It is not meant to be fair. We are beyond epic now, beyond romance and beyond the fairy-tale ending. In the real world things seldom turn out as we would like them to, and the little man is as subject to tragedy as the great one.

> —*Verlyn Flieger, "Frodo and Aragorn: The Concept of Hero in 'The Lord of the Ring,'" in Isaacs and Zimbardo, eds.,* Tolkien: New Critical Perspectives, *1981*

On Tolkien's Christianity

The Lord of the Rings, then, although it presents no "God," no "Christ," and no "Christians," embodies much of Tolkien's "real religion" and is a profoundly Christian work. No "God" is required in this story. . . . Gandalf and Aragorn need not turn our thoughts to . . . Christ . . . but they persuade us that if we are to have hope in our lives and in our history it must be hope for the kind of power and authority revealed in Aragorn the king and on the basis of the kind of power revealed in Gandalf's "miracles" and in his rising from the dead. What Frodo does and undergoes speaks to us of what a man's responsibility, according to the Christian faith, must always be: to renounce the kind of power which would enslave others and ourselves and to submit to that power which frees us all.

—*Gunnar Urang, "Tolkien's Fantasy: The Phenomenology of Hope," in Mark R. Hillegas, ed.,* Shadows of the Imagination, *1969*

On Hobbits

His Hobbit is both a bridge and a being more like Man than are the heroic, familiar, mock-human counterparts that appear in adventure stories. Moreover, the hobbit is . . . more of a human than if he were one, as petit-bourgeois as if he caught the 8:15 commuter train. . . .

The rather jolly virtues of the Hobbits are raised to solemn magnificence when it is realized that these virtues endow their possessors with the power to face and subdue the terrible and soul-destroying opposition of Evil that besets them. It is the reluctant choice to face or not to face Evil . . . that raised Bilbo and more so his heir Frodo, above even great Beowulf.

—*William Ready,* The Tolkien Relation, *1968*

A Detractor's View

What we get is a simple confrontation—in more or less the traditional terms of British melodrama—of the Forces of Evil with the Forces of Good, the remote and alien villain with the plucky little home-grown hero. . . . For the most part such characterizations as Dr. Tolkien has been able to contrive are perfectly stereotyped: Frodo the good little Englishman, Samwise, his doglike servant, who talks lower class and respectful, and who never deserts his master. These characters . . . are involved in interminable adventures the poverty of invention displayed in which is . . . almost pathetic.

> —*Edmund Wilson, "Oo, Those*
> *Awful Orcs!" in* The Nation,
> *April 14, 1956*